creating
a web page
in dreamweaver 8

Visual QuickProject Guide

by Nolan Hester

**Peachpit
Press**

Visual QuickProject Guide

Creating a Web Page in Dreamweaver 8

Nolan Hester

Peachpit Press

1249 Eighth Street
Berkeley, CA 94710
510/524-2178
800/283-9444
510/524-2221 (fax)

Find us on the World Wide Web at: www.peachpit.com
To report errors, please send a note to errata@peachpit.com
Peachpit Press is a division of Pearson Education

Editor: Nancy Davis
Production Editor: Lisa Brazieal
Compositor: David Van Ness
Proofreader: Tracy D. O'Connell
Screenshot assistance: Ann Navarro
Indexer: FireCrystal Communications
Cover design: Peachpit Press, Aren Howell
Interior design: Elizabeth Castro
Interior photos: Ali Pearson and Shannon Smith
Cover photo credit: iStockPhoto

Notice of Rights

Notice of Liability

Trademarks

ISBN 0-321-37022-8

9 8 7 6 5 4 3 2 1

Printed and bound in the United States of America

To Mary, for helping create this life of startling delight.

Special Thanks to...

Nancy Davis, my editor, without whom this book would be not nearly so good — or fun,

David Van Ness for setting the pace and the standards,

Emily Glossbrenner of FireCrystal for yet another superior index,

Terry Wardwell for creating Tuffits,

Marjorie Baer and Cary Norsworthy for helping me get the first edition of this book off the ground,

And Nancy Aldrich-Ruenzel, Peachpit's publisher, for making this work-from-home life possible.

contents

contents

introduction

The Visual QuickProject Guide that you hold in your hands offers a unique way to learn about new technologies. Instead of drowning you in theoretical possibilities and lengthy explanations, this Visual QuickProject Guide uses big, color illustrations coupled with clear, concise step-by-step instructions to show you how to complete one specific project in a matter of hours.

Our project in this book is to create a beautiful Web site using Macromedia Dreamweaver 8, one of the best programs for building Web sites. Our Web site displays the products for a real company that makes cast concrete stepping stones that look like couch pillows. Because the project covers all the techniques needed to build a basic Web site, you'll be able to use what you learn to create your own Web site. Thanks to Dreamweaver, you'll do all this without having to enter a single line of HTML, the code that drives the Web.

what you'll create

These two pages represent just some of the things you'll learn to create.

Format text and headings in the font, size, and colors you want. (See page 12.)

Add images and wrap text around them. (See page 33.)

Create a site-wide navigation bar to guide visitors as they explore your site. (See page 107.)

Reduce and resample images to make them quicker to download. (See page 40.)

Create internal, external, and email links, then give them a consistent appearance using external style sheets. (See pages 61 and 75.)

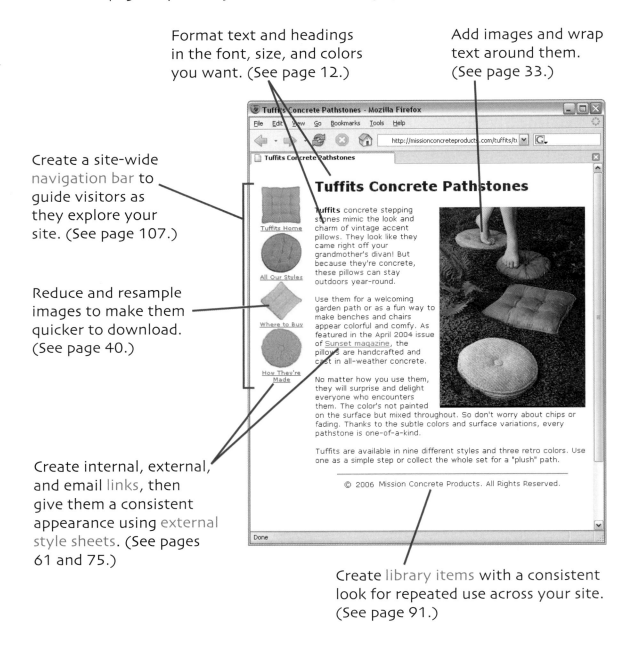

Create library items with a consistent look for repeated use across your site. (See page 91.)

Build tables for displaying everything from images to tabular data. (See page 47.)

Create image maps that link specific parts of images to different files. (See page 86.)

Apply colors and formatting to tables to make them easier to read. (See page 57.)

Sort data alphabetically or numerically within a table's columns or rows. (See page 58.)

Create anchor links so readers can jump to the right spot in a long document. (See page 83.)

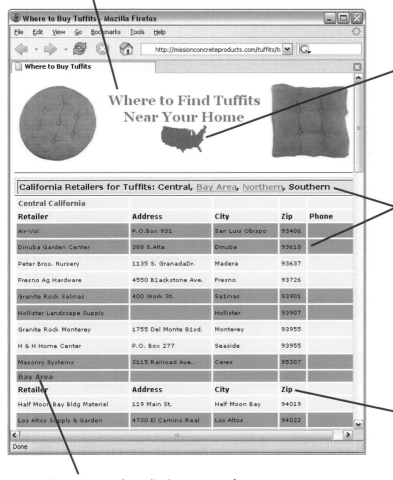

how this book works

The title explains what is covered in that section.

Names of Dreamweaver elements, file names, and other important concepts are shown in orange.

add image to table

Tables are great for organizing large amounts of text and data, but adding a picture or two will make them more appealing. (See extra bits on page 60.)

Numbered steps lead you through the sequence of actions, showing only the details you really need.

1 Click in the first cell of the table you just created and from the Menu bar, choose Insert > Image.

2 In the Select Image Source dialog box, open your site's Images folder.

Screenshots focus on what part of Dreamweaver you'll be using for that particular project step.

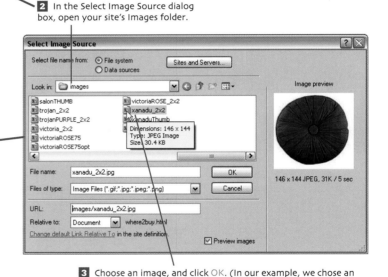

3 Choose an image, and click OK. (In our example, we chose an image of one of the Tuffits pillows.) When the Image Tab Accessibility Attributes dialog box appears, type in Alternate text for the image. (For more information, see add image on page 35.) Repeat steps 1–3 to insert another image in the far-right cell.

50   **add tables**

The extra bits section at the end of each chapter contains additional tips and tricks that you might like to know—but that aren't absolutely necessary for creating the Web page.

import tabular data

extra bits

add a table p. 40

- Use the Table dialog box's Accessibility section to create an explanatory Caption that will be read aloud by special audio Web browsers for visually impaired visitors. If needed, add details in the Summary field.

add image to table p. 50

- If you're having trouble selecting a table, click near the table and then press Ctrl A in Windows or ⌘ A on the Mac. Or click the < table > tag down in the status bar.
- For more precision in resizing the table, type a number into the W field of the Properties inspector and press Tab.

add labels p. 52

- The Table dialog box Header options—None, Left, Top, and Both—let you skip adding labels, label only the rows, label only the columns, or label both rows and columns.

import tabular data p. 54

- Before importing, use your spreadsheet or word-processing program to save the data in comma- or tab-delimited form.
- Sometimes the Set drop-down menu in the Table Width section of the Import Tabular Data dialog box will switch to Percent—even if you previously set it to Pixels. So double-check before clicking OK.
- Our copy-and-paste example works because each table had the same number of columns. You cannot, for example, copy 6 columns and paste them into 4 columns.

format table colors p. 57

- By using Ctrl-click in Windows or ⌘-click on the Mac, you also can select non-adjacent columns or cells. Then you can format all the selections at once.

sort tables p. 58

- By default, the Options in the Sort Table dialog box are not checked, since you seldom want the header or footer rows sorted.

The heading for each group of tips matches the section title. (The colors are just for decoration and have no hidden meaning.)

Next to the heading there's a page number that also shows which section the tips belong to.

60   add tables

the web site

You can find this book's companion site at http://www.waywest.net/dwvqj/.

You'll find all the example files used in the book, including the images.

You'll also find extra tips on working with Dreamweaver, plus corrections if any mistakes are found.

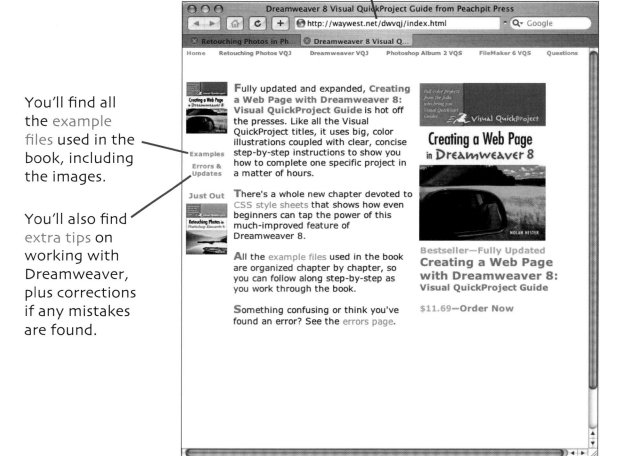

useful tools

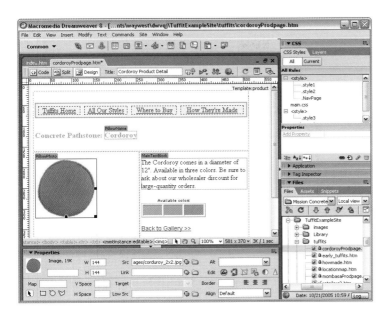

Naturally, you'll need a computer, and you'll need Dreamweaver 8, which is packed with most of the tools you'll need, including a way to publish to the Web.

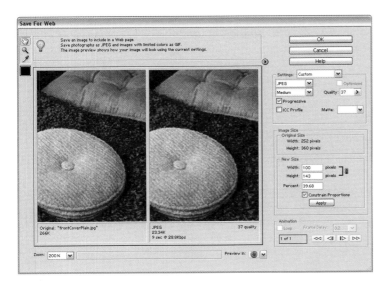

You'll also need an image editor. If you bought Dreamweaver as part of Macromedia Studio 8, then you'll be able to use Fireworks, which is a full-fledged image editor designed to work hand-in-hand with Dreamweaver. Your digital camera may have included an image-editing program. Other-wise, consider Adobe Photoshop Elements, which also contains specific tools for working with Web images.

the next step

While this Visual QuickProject Guide gives you a good start on creating a Web site using Dreamweaver, there is a lot more to learn. If you want to dive into all the details, try Macromedia Dreamweaver 8 for Windows and Macintosh: Visual QuickStart Guide, by Tom Negrino and Dori Smith.

Chapter 2

Cloaking Files

Not every folder in your local site needs to be uploaded to the remote site on the Web server. Dreamweaver allows folders to be *cloaked*, which means that they will be exempt from synchronization. This can save you a lot of time. Imagine that you're working on a site that contains large movie files. Cloaking the folder that contains the movie files means that while you're working on other parts of the site, Dreamweaver won't take the time to scan through the folders when synchronizing, and won't upload any of the files. When you're ready to upload the files, uncloak the movies folder and synchronize the local and remote sites.

To cloak a site folder:

1. Right-click a folder in the files area.

2. From the resulting shortcut menu, choose the Cloaking submenu, then from the submenu, choose Cloak (**Figure 2.23**). Dreamweaver displays the folder with a slash through it, indicating that it is cloaked.

✔ **Tip**

■ You can only cloak folders; you can't cloak individual files. But you *can* cloak all files of a particular type. Choose Site > Manage Sites, then select the site you're working on. In the Advanced tab of the Site Definition dialog, choose the Cloaking category. Enable the "Cloak files ending with" check box, then enter the file extensions of the kinds of files you want to cloak (**Figure 2.24**).

To uncloak a site folder:

1. Right-click a cloaked folder in the files area.

2. From the resulting shortcut menu, choose Cloaking > Uncloak or Cloaking > Uncloak All.

Figure 2.23 Choosing Cloak from the Files panel shortcut menu keeps a folder and its contents from being affected during synchronization operations.

Figure 2.24 The Cloaking category in the Site Definition dialog allows you to set particular kinds of files to always be cloaked.

The Macromedia Dreamweaver 8: Visual QuickStart Guide features clear examples, concise step-by-step instructions, and tons of helpful tips. With more than 500 pages, it covers darn near every aspect of Dreamweaver.

1. welcome to dreamweaver

Macromedia Dreamweaver is a powerful program, packed with cool features to create Web sites. So packed, in fact, that it can be a bit overwhelming.

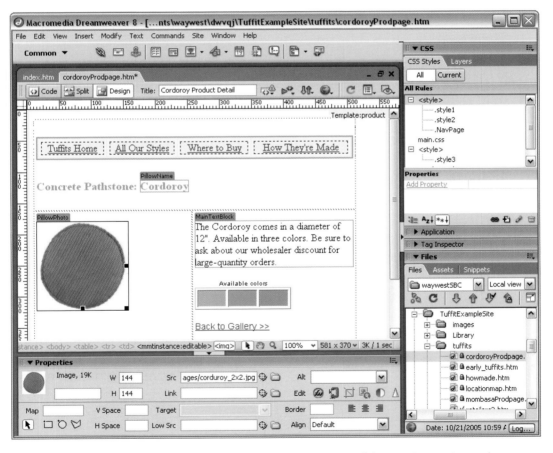

Not to worry. We aren't going to explain every possible option—just the crucial ones to keep you going, no matter how daunting Dreamweaver may seem initially. We'll have some fun along the way, too, so let's get started.

explore dreamweaver

A series of key toolbars, windows, and panels surrounds your main Dreamweaver document. Take a moment to understand how all of these tools work and you'll save yourself frustration later. (See extra bits on page 8.)

When you open more than one file, a series of tabs appears across the top of the main window to indicate which ones are open.

The current file's title appears at the center of the toolbar, followed by some buttons related to posting your site on the Web. Use the last button if you want to see a ruler or grid while building pages.

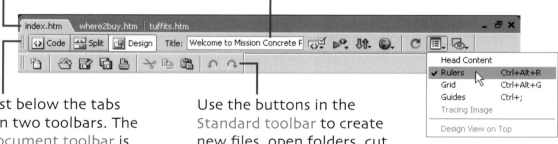

Just below the tabs run two toolbars. The Document toolbar is set by default to the Design view. You can change it to show only the Code view or use the Split view to show the Code and Design views.

Use the buttons in the Standard toolbar to create new files, open folders, cut and paste, save files, and undo actions.

Depending on what you're doing, switch the Insert toolbar to display the relevant buttons using the drop-down menu. (To show or hide the toolbar, in the Menu bar choose Window > Insert.)

Many of the toolbar's buttons have their own drop-down menus.

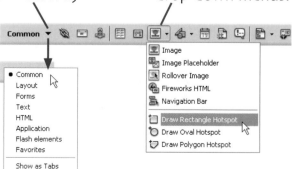

welcome to dreamweaver

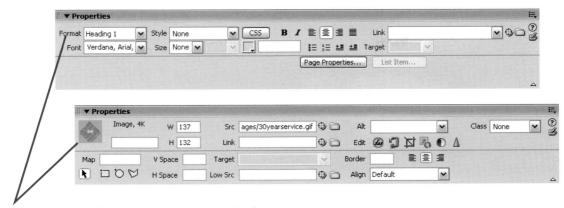

Depending on what you've selected, the Properties inspector changes to display the relevant information and tools, such as those for text or images. To see or hide the inspector, press Ctrl F3 .

With two tabs containing all your Files and Assets, the Files panel offers an essential view of your Web site. To open the panel, press F8 .

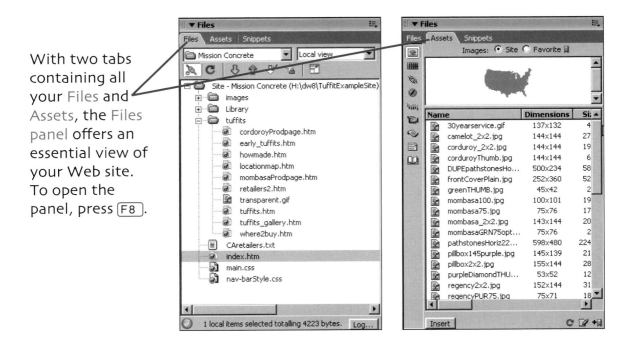

set up local site

Once you've installed Dreamweaver, your first step is to set up a local version of your Web site on your computer. (See extra bits on page 8.)

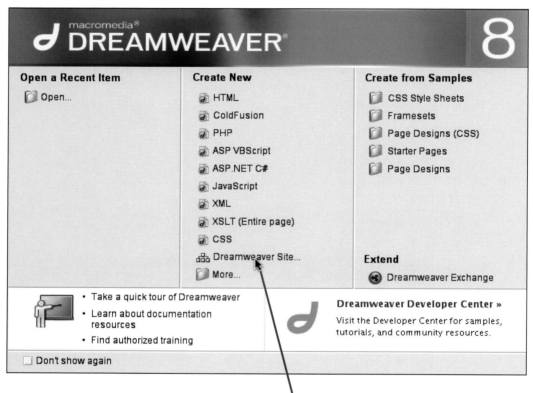

1 Launch Dreamweaver and when the Start Page appears, click the Dreamweaver Site button.

2 Dreamweaver automatically assigns a generic name to your new site and highlights it.

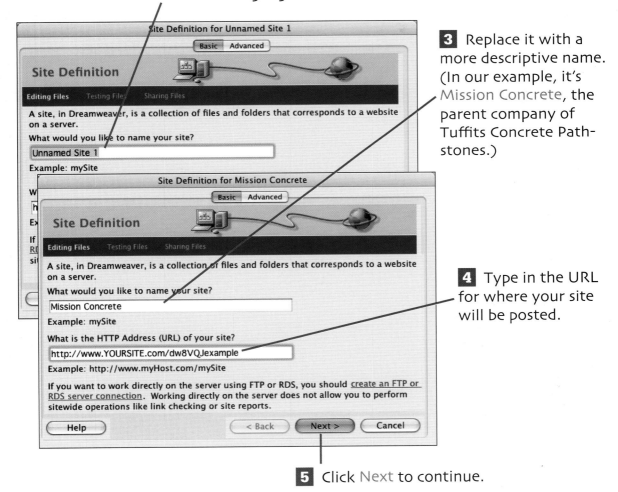

3 Replace it with a more descriptive name. (In our example, it's Mission Concrete, the parent company of Tuffits Concrete Path-stones.)

4 Type in the URL for where your site will be posted.

5 Click Next to continue.

set up local site (cont.)

6 When the next Site Definition window appears, choose No and click Next.

7 In the next window, choose Edit local copies on my machine.

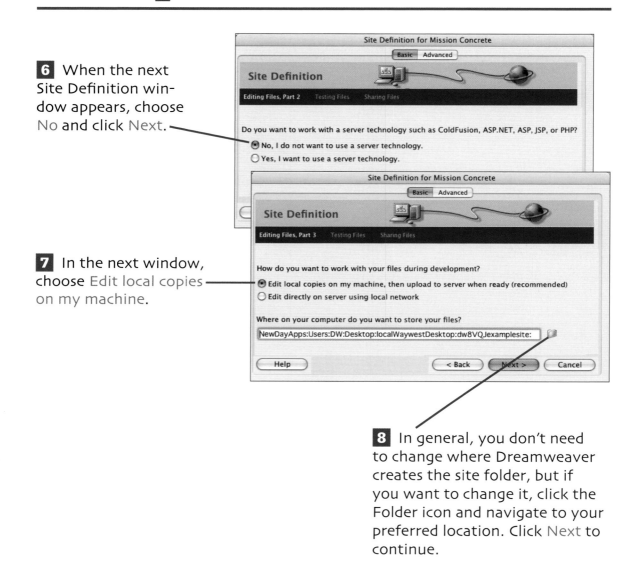

8 In general, you don't need to change where Dreamweaver creates the site folder, but if you want to change it, click the Folder icon and navigate to your preferred location. Click Next to continue.

9 In the next window, choose FTP from the drop-down menu.

10 Fill in the FTP address for your new site, based on information provided by the firm that will be hosting your site.

11 You don't have to specify which folder will contain the site, but it can help keep your site better organized. (In our example, we've created a special folder, dw8VQJexample, for storing this book's example files.)

12 Fill in your login and password, again based on the information from your Web host.

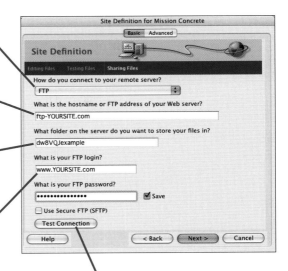

13 Assuming you're already online, click Test Connection and it will take only a moment for Dreamweaver to determine if the connection's working. Click Next to continue.

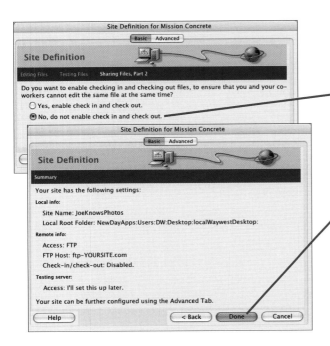

14 When the next Site Definition window appears, choose No, do not enable check in and check out and click Next.

15 Double-check the Summary information before clicking Done. You're ready to build your site. See create a basic home page on page 9.

welcome to dreamweaver

extra bits

explore dreamweaver p. 2

- Unless you're familiar with HTML or CSS coding, leave the toolbar set to Design.

- Rather than explain every tool and button here, we'll cover them in the coming chapters as we need them. We also don't cover items more suited to experienced users, such as the Files panel's Snippets tab, which can store frequently used bits of code.

- You also can see or hide the contents of any panel by clicking the triangle-shaped arrow at the upper left of the panel.

- Using Dreamweaver's keyboard shortcuts (provided by Macromedia) greatly speeds your work.

  To download the Windows shortcuts, go to: http://download.macromedia.com/pub/documentation/en/dreamweaver/dw8/dw8_shortcuts_Win.pdf.

  To download the Mac shortcuts, go to: http://download.macromedia.com/pub/documentation/en/dreamweaver/dw8/dw8_shortcuts_Mac.pdf.

set up local site p. 4

- The name you enter in the Site Definition window only appears within Dreamweaver, not on your actual Web site. Pick one to distinguish this site from the many others you'll no doubt be creating soon.

- Web-hosting firms usually email you a login name and password for posting your files. Keep the original email where you won't delete it and can find it later. If you ever buy a new computer, you'll need that password because Dreamweaver never reveals the password, just those black dots.

- If the test connection fails, double-check your entries in the Site Definition window. Note that entries are case sensitive. Almost inevitably, you'll find a mistyped entry.

- Use the check-in system only if there are several people building the Web site; it keeps you from overwriting each other's work.

2. create a basic home page

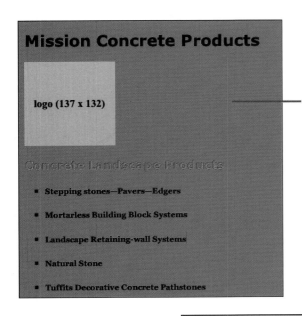

As the front door to your Web site, the home page invites visitors to step in and take a look around. In this chapter, you'll build a simple home page to quickly orient visitors to what your site offers. In later chapters, you'll learn to dress it up a bit with images and some special features. Here, however, we'll focus on the basics: creating, naming, titling, and saving this all-important page.

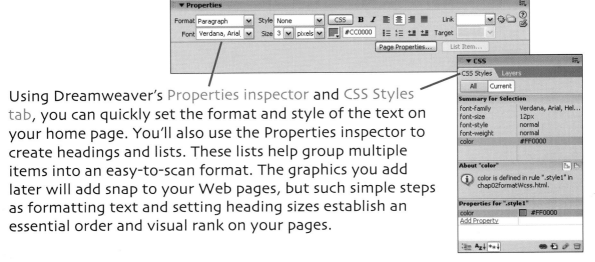

Using Dreamweaver's Properties inspector and CSS Styles tab, you can quickly set the format and style of the text on your home page. You'll also use the Properties inspector to create headings and lists. These lists help group multiple items into an easy-to-scan format. The graphics you add later will add snap to your Web pages, but such simple steps as formatting text and setting heading sizes establish an essential order and visual rank on your pages.

create your home page

The mechanics of making your home page are pretty simple. The first step is to create a new page, then name the file, give it a title, and save it. While you can give the home page any title you wish, try to use something that helps visitors immediately understand your site's purpose. If you have not already done so, launch Dreamweaver, and the site you created in Chapter 1 opens by default. (See extra bits on page 31.)

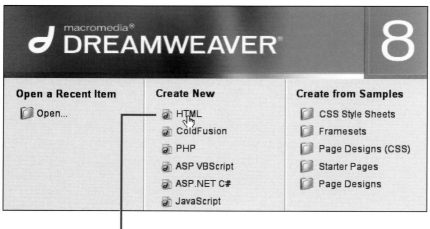

If you're using Dreamweaver's Start Page, click the HTML button in the Create New column.

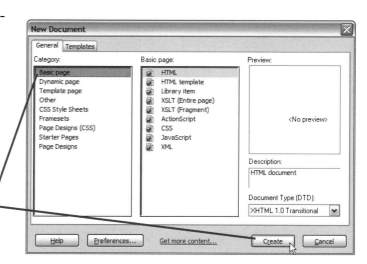

Or, using the Menu bar, choose File > New. When the New Document dialog box appears, use the General tab to select Basic page (HTML will be selected automatically) and click Create.

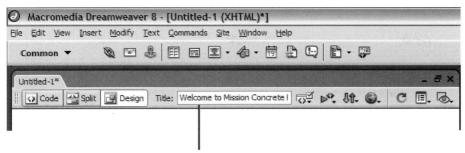

When a new untitled page appears in Dreamweaver's main window, click inside the Title text window, and type in your own title for the page. (Our sample site uses Welcome to Mission Concrete Products.) Visitors to your site will see the title at the top of their browser window, where it acts as a label for your site. It's not the same as the page's file name.

From the Menu bar, choose File > Save. In the Save As dialog box that opens, navigate to the site folder you created in Chapter 1. This will be your home page, so name it index and click Save. (Dreamweaver automatically adds the appropriate .htm or .html suffix.) The page will be saved and appear as part of your site in Dreamweaver's Files tab. (Dreamweaver automatically generates the logs, images, and cgi folders.)

create a basic home page

add text

Adding text to your Web page in Dreamweaver is not that different from using a word processing program, with the exception of using certain special characters explained in step 4. (See extra bits on page 31.)

1 Click anywhere in your still-blank home page and type the first line of text. In our example, the company name, Mission Concrete Products, is the first thing we want the viewer to see.

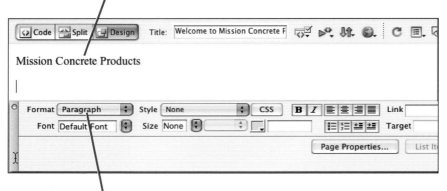

2 Press [Enter] (Windows) or [Return] (Mac) to start a new paragraph, just as you would with a word processing program. You'll see in the Properties inspector that Dreamweaver automatically applies the Paragraph format to the text.

create a basic home page

3 Type in the rest of your text, setting off each line as a separate paragraph (Enter in Windows, Return on the Mac). In our example, we've entered Concrete Landscape Products and Stepping Stones.

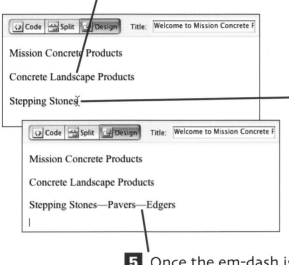

4 Unlike with word processing programs, certain characters cannot be typed directly into a Web page. In our example, we want to add an em-dash right after the word Stones. Choose Insert > HTML > Special Characters, and choose from the drop-down menu to trigger the insertion.

5 Once the em-dash is inserted, we can add the rest of the text, including a second em-dash.

6 Save your changes by choosing File > Save. In a moment, we'll use the Properties inspector to create headings and lists with some of this text. But first we want to insert a placeholder for the image we'll eventually add in Chapter 3.

create a basic home page

insert image placeholder

In a perfect world, all your images would be ready to put into your Web pages right when you're building them. In reality, someone else may be creating the image even though you need to get started building pages. That's why I explain inserting an image placeholder right in the middle of this text-building chapter. You always can add the image later (as explained in Chapter 3), but this trick lets you keep working.

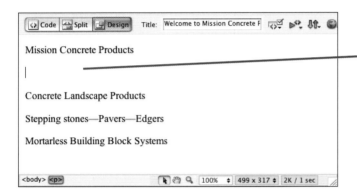

Open a page and click in the text exactly where you expect to eventually place an image. In our example, we're waiting for the company logo for the home page.

From the Menu bar, choose Insert > Image Objects > Image Placeholder. Type in a memory-jogging name for the image-to-come. If you know the image's exact width and height in pixels, type it in. Otherwise, enter an approximate size. Finally, enter Alternate text that briefly describes the image or its function. (For more on Alt text see page 45.) Click OK to close the dialog box.

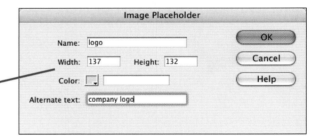

create a basic home page

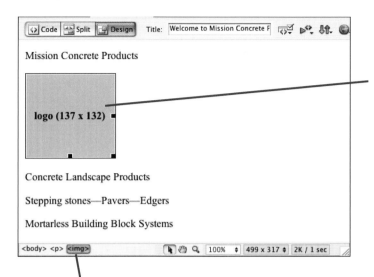

Dreamweaver inserts a box into the Web page based on your chosen width and height, helping you gauge how the page will look— and, most importantly, reminding you that you're still missing an image.

Down in the status bar, the tag selector inserts an HTML image tag < img >, where previously there only had been body and paragraph tags. The tag selector will prove handy later on when we begin styling items on the page.

create headings

Just like newspaper and magazine headlines, headings on a Web page are larger and more noticeable than regular text. They range from size 1 (the largest) to size 6 (the smallest). Use larger sizes for more important items and smaller sizes for less important items. (See extra bits on page 32.)

Select the first line of text in your home page (Mission Concrete Products in our sample project). In the Properties inspector, select Heading 1 from the Format drop-down menu.

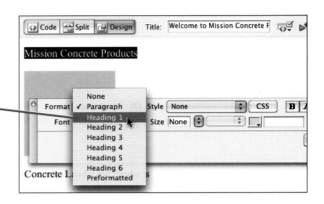

The selected line changes from regular text to the larger, bolder Heading 1.

Down in the status bar, the tag selector inserts the new heading tag < h1 >.

create a basic home page

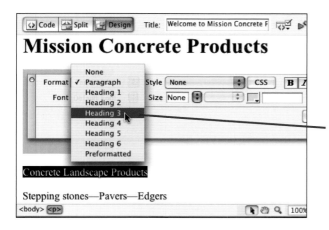

Select the second line (Concrete Landscape Products) and in the Properties inspector, select Heading 3 from the Format drop-down menu.

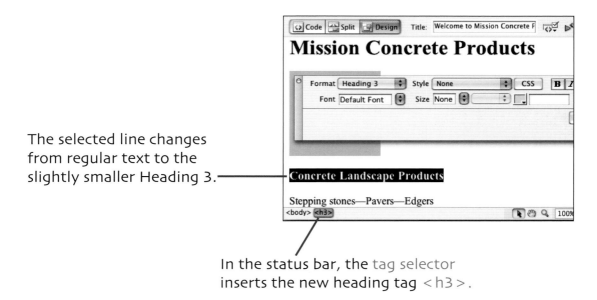

The selected line changes from regular text to the slightly smaller Heading 3.

In the status bar, the tag selector inserts the new heading tag < h3 >.

create headings (cont.)

Click and drag your cursor to select the next five lines, which in our example lists various Mission Concrete products. In the Properties inspector, select Heading 5 from the Format drop-down menu.

All the lines become smaller and the tag selector inserts the new heading tag <h5>. The smaller size suggests that the items in these five lines are types of products falling within the Concrete Landscape Products heading. To make that distinction even clearer, however, the next section shows how to format the products as a list. Save your changes by choosing File > Save (Ctrl S in Windows, ⌘S on the Mac).

create lists

Organizing information into lists, whether numbered or simply marked with bullets, makes it easy to group lots of items in a way that anyone can instantly recognize. Ordered lists are great when you need to highlight a specific sequence of steps or materials. We'll quickly show you how to do ordered and unordered lists.

logo (137 x 132)

Concrete Landscape Products

Stepping stones—Pavers—Edgers

Mortarless Building Block Systems

Landscape Retaining-wall Systems

Natural Stone

Tuffits Decorative Concrete Pathstones

Return to your home page and select lines 3–7 on the home page. If it's not already visible, open the Properties inspector (Window > Properties) and click the Ordered List icon, just above the Page Properties button.

`<body>`   100%   532 x 437   2K / 1 sec

Format Heading 5   Style None   CSS **B** *I*
Font Default Font   Size None

Page Properties.

Concrete Landscape Products

1. Stepping stones—Pavers—Edgers

2. Mortarless Building Block Systems

3. Landscape Retaining-wall Systems

4. Natural Stone

5. Tuffits Decorative Concrete Pathstones

The selected lines will be numbered in sequence from 1 to 5 below the larger Concrete Landscape Products heading.

`<body> <ol> <li> <h5>`   100%   532 x 437   2K / 1 sec

Format Heading 5   Style None   CSS **B** *I*
Font Default Font   Size None

Page Properties.

create lists (cont.)

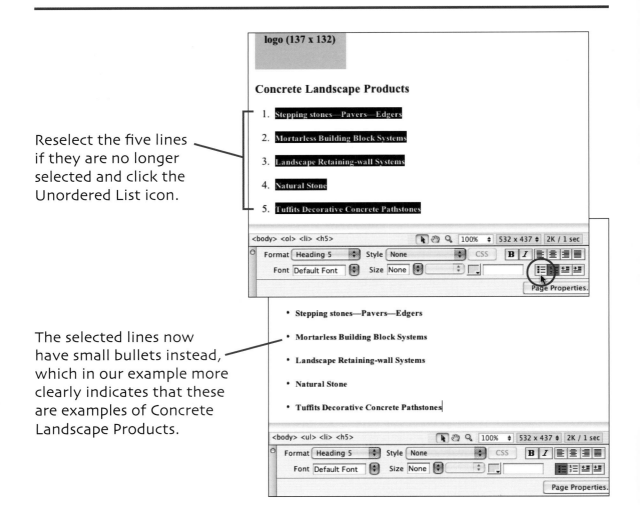

Reselect the five lines if they are no longer selected and click the Unordered List icon.

The selected lines now have small bullets instead, which in our example more clearly indicates that these are examples of Concrete Landscape Products.

Save your changes (Ctrl S in Windows, ⌘ S on the Mac).

set page background

You often see Web pages that use background images behind the text. Many of these pages use what's called a tiled image, where a small image is repeated across the page. Others use a single large image. In either case, unless the image is a very simple one, it can make it hard to read the page's text. Instead of adding an image, you can simply change the page's background from the default white to a color that makes your home page pop—without giving your visitors a headache.

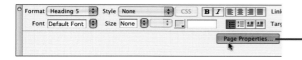

Click the Page Properties button in the Properties inspector.

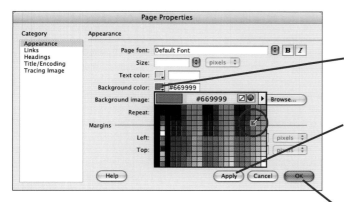

In the Page Properties dialog box, click the Background color drop-down menu and pick a color that provides good contrast with your text color.

Click Apply to see the page color change. To try another color, click the Background color drop-down menu again. Once you're happy with your choice, click OK to close the Page Properties dialog box.

Mission Concrete Products

logo (137 x 132)

Concrete Landscape Products

- Stepping stones—Pavers—Edgers

- Mortarless Building Block Systems

- Landscape Retaining-wall Systems

- Natural Stone

- Tuffits Decorative Concrete Pathstones

Dreamweaver applies your changes to your home page. Save your changes.

create CSS rules

NEW In previous versions of Dreamweaver, the Properties inspector served as the main tool to format and style text. As we showed in the previous section, it still makes sense to use the inspector to create headings and lists. As of now, however, all other formatting tasks should be done using the more powerful CSS Styles tab. Using CSS (Cascading Style Sheets) also makes it much easier to reuse styles and update them across your Web site. (See extra bits on page 32.)

Open your home page (Mission Concrete Products in our sample project) and open the CSS Styles tab (from the Menu bar, choose Window > CSS Styles) if it's not already visible in the right-hand panels.

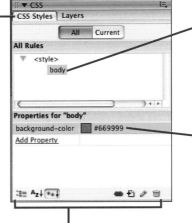

At the moment, the only CSS rule is body, which was created when you set the page's background color on page 21. That background-color (#669999) is listed as a property for the body rule in the bottom half of the CSS Styles tab.

Icons for switching views and changing the rules, which we'll use as we need them, run across the bottom of the tab.

create a basic home page

In the main window, select a Heading 1 line of text (in our example, Mission Concrete Products) and click the New CSS Rule button in the CSS Styles tab.

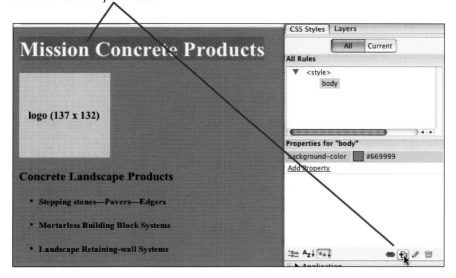

In the New CSS Rule dialog box, select Tag, which we'll use to define a specific tag—in this case the h1 tag already applied to the text.

Because of that prior formatting, the Tag field will display h1 automatically.

Select This document only and click OK to close the dialog box.

create a basic home page

A blank CSS Rule definition dialog box for the h1 tag opens. Click the Font drop-down menu and choose Verdana, Arial, Helvetica, sans-serif. The six font groups listed in the drop-down menu are found on nearly every computer, ensuring that your Web visitors will see a font similar to what you're seeing.

Set the Size drop-down menu to 24 and the Style drop-down menu to normal. Click OK to close the dialog box.

The selected line immediately reflects the new properties for the h1 style, which are listed in the bottom half of the CSS Styles tab.

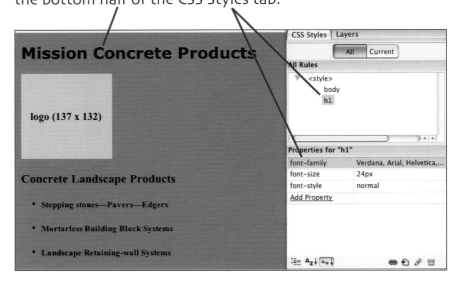

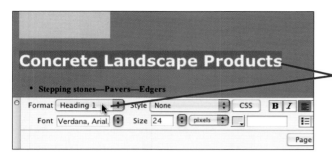

Having defined the Heading 1 style with the CSS Styles tab, you can apply that same formatting elsewhere just by selecting text and choosing Heading 1 in the Properties inspector. In our example, we've done just that to Concrete Landscape Products, which had been formatted as a Heading 3.

Since we actually want to create a particular Heading 3 style, we'll return Concrete Landscape Products to its previous format by selecting the line and choosing Heading 3 from the Format drop-down menu.

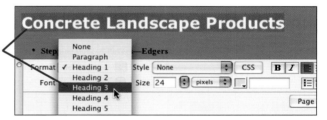

Leave Concrete Landscape Products selected and click the New CSS Rule button in the CSS Styles tab.

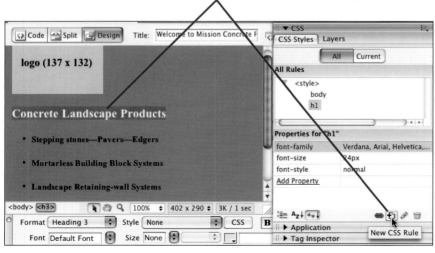

create CSS rules (cont.)

In the New CSS Rule dialog box, Tag will already be selected, with the Tag field set to h3, and This document only will already be selected. Click OK to close the dialog box.

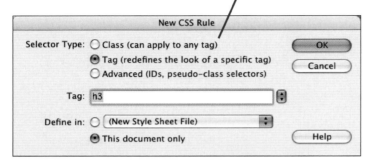

In the CSS Rule definition dialog box, click the Font drop-down menu and choose Verdana, Arial, Helvetica, sans-serif. Set the Size to 18, the Weight to bold, use the Color drop-down menu to choose a strong red (#CC0000), and click OK to close the dialog box.

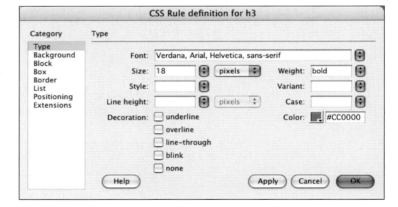

create a basic home page

The selected line (Concrete Landscape Products) immediately reflects the new properties for the h3 style.

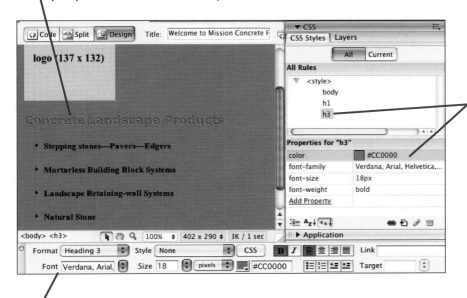

The new h3 rule is now listed in the top part of the CSS Styles tab, with its properties listed in the bottom half.

The Properties inspector also displays the same properties for Heading 3, allowing you to apply them to anything else you format as a Heading 3.

create a basic home page

create CSS rules (cont.)

Quickly create one last CSS rule by selecting any of the Heading 5 text and clicking the New CSS Rule button. The dialog box automatically sets itself to create a Tag for h5 for This document only, so click OK to move to the next step.

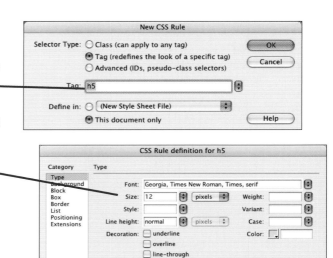

In the CSS Rule definition dialog box, choose Georgia, Times New Roman, Times, serif from the Font drop-down menu, set the Size to 12, the Line height to normal, and click OK to close the dialog box.

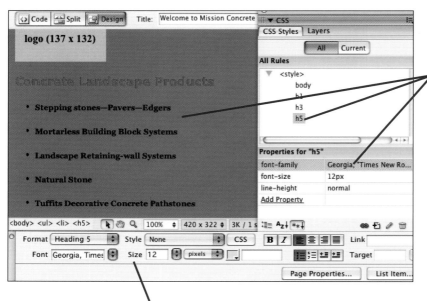

The Heading 5 text now reflects the new properties with the new h5 rule added to the top of the CSS Styles tab and its properties listed in the bottom half.

The Properties inspector also displays the new Heading 5 properties.

Save your work before going to the next page.

create a basic home page

change CSS rules

NEW The real beauty of using CSS rules for headings, lists, and other text becomes obvious when you need to make a change. In this example, we'll deliberately make a mistake and show how easy it is to fix.

Start by selecting the unordered list we first created for the home page on page 19. To quickly select a list, click < ul > (for unordered list) in the tag selector within the status bar. The entire list is highlighted.

Click the New CSS Rule button in the CSS Styles tab and when the New CSS rule dialog box appears, Tag will already be selected, with the Tag field set to ul, and This document only selected. Click OK to close the dialog box.

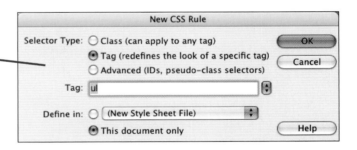

In the CSS Rule definition dialog box, click List in the Category field, then set Type to square, Position to inside, and click OK to close the dialog box.

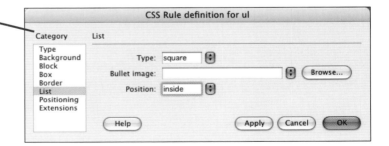

change CSS rules (cont.)

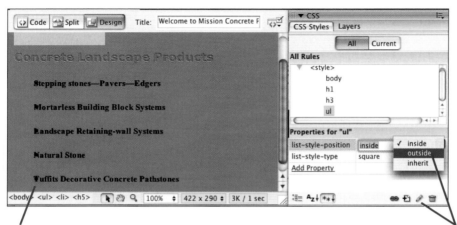

Whoops, obviously that inside setting isn't what we want for this list.

To change all the list's properties, we could click the pencil button to open the rule definition dialog box. But since we just want to change one setting, we can fix it within the Properties portion of the CSS Styles tab. To change the list-style-position, click the inside property and select outside from the drop-down menu.

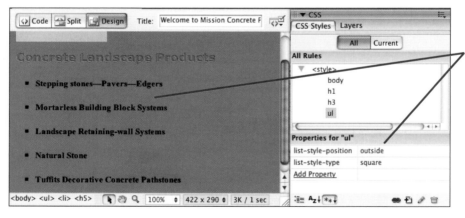

The unordered list now puts the bullets where we want them and the Properties portion of the CSS Styles tab reflects the change.

Save your work ([Ctrl][S] in Windows, [⌘][S] on the Mac) before turning to the next chapter where we'll add graphics to your pages.

create a basic home page

extra bits

create your home page p. 10

- The page's file name and title serve different purposes. The file name is used behind the scenes to help you and Dreamweaver keep track of how your files are organized. For example, home pages should always be named index, which helps Web servers know that this page is the "front door" to your site. The page title is what the viewer's Web browser displays when your page is onscreen.

- The Basic Page column offers lots of choices, including templates and library items. Both are explained in later chapters (see pages 91 and 96). Working with non-HTML pages, such as those using CSS and XML, is covered in the Macromedia Dreamweaver 8: Visual QuickStart Guide.

- NEW Catching up with the default view in previous Windows versions, Mac users now can display all their Dreamweaver 8 pages (even single pages) as tabs in the main window. Choose Edit > Preferences > General (Windows) or Dreamweaver > Preferences > General (Mac) and in Document options check Always show tabs.

add text p. 12

- Macintosh computers display Web page text at about three-fourths the size that it appears on a Windows machine, so if you are building your Web site on a Windows PC, avoid the smallest text sizes. On the other hand, if you're creating pages with a Mac, leave enough space at the bottom of text columns to handle the text running about 25 percent longer when viewed on a Windows machine.

- When you first choose a special character, a dialog box warns that it may not be available for non-Western alphabets. Click OK to continue.

- To see all 99 special characters that are available, choose Insert > HTML > Special Characters > Other.

- To reach the special characters more easily, switch the Insert bar from Common to Text, then click the far-right button and choose from the drop-down menu.

extra bits

create headings p. 16

- To keep your pages uncluttered, limit yourself to no more than two or three heading sizes on the same page.

create CSS rules p. 22

- While you can choose Edit Font List in the Font drop-down menu and pick a particular font installed on your own computer, there's no guarantee visitors will have the font, so stick to the six most common font groups.

- For now, we're creating CSS rules for this page only. But as you'll see in Chapter 5, we can use them to quickly create rules for an entire Web site.

create a basic home page

3. add images

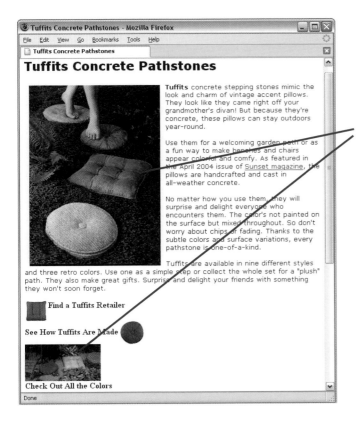

While text and headlines lend structure and meaning to Web pages, it's images that give your pages real impact.

Dreamweaver can handle basic image editing; for more demanding tasks use a dedicated graphics program. If you don't already have a graphics program, take a look in the graphics section of www.versiontracker.com where you can compare prices, features, and user comments.

image tools

As with text-related tasks, the Properties inspector acts as your main tool for most image work. (See extra bits on page 45.)

Displayed near the image thumbnail is the file size (52K in our example) and its W (width) and H (height) in pixels.

Src tells you where the image is stored, while Link tells you what file (if any) the image is linked to if clicked.

Alt lets you create a label to be read aloud by browsers created for visually handi-capped visitors. Also use Alt to describe an image for visitors who have turned off image downloading for speedier surfing.

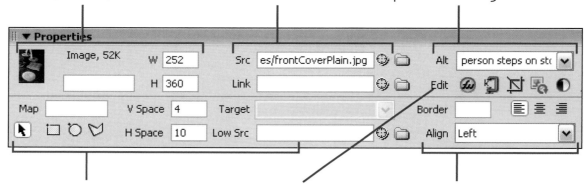

The items from Map to Target are used to create image maps, as explained on pages 85–86.

Some of the Edit buttons only work if you have installed Macromedia Fire-works. Without Fireworks, you're limited to using the Crop, Contrast/Brightness, and Sharpen buttons (see pages 37, 39, and 41).

Use Border to set the border width around the image. The three but-tons to the right control whether your image is set at the left, center, or right of the page. Use the Align drop-down menu to control how text wraps around the image (see pages 42–44).

add image

After preparing images in an external program, you're ready to add them to your Web pages. (See extra bits on page 45.)

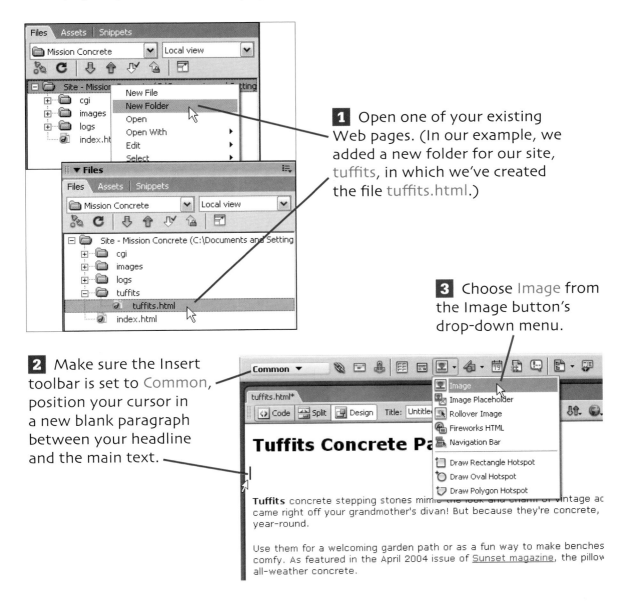

1 Open one of your existing Web pages. (In our example, we added a new folder for our site, tuffits, in which we've created the file tuffits.html.)

3 Choose Image from the Image button's drop-down menu.

2 Make sure the Insert toolbar is set to Common, position your cursor in a new blank paragraph between your headline and the main text.

add image (cont.)

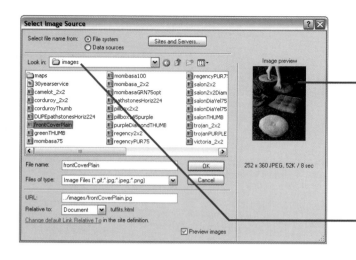

4 When the Select Image Source dialog box appears, navigate to the image you want to use (using the preview area to help you choose), and click OK.

5 If the image isn't already a part of your Web site, Dreamweaver asks if you want to save it in the site's root folder. Choose Yes, navigate to your site's images, and save the image there. The selected image appears between the headline and the main text.

6 Once inserted on the page, the image remains selected, so click the align center button in the Properties inspector to center the image on the page.

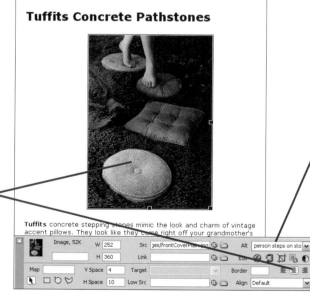

7 Type a brief description of the image in the Alt text box. Save the page before continuing.

crop image

You don't need a separate graphics program for cropping images—just don't use your original image. Cropping permanently alters your image, so if you make a mistake, immediately choose Undo Crop in the Edit menu. (See extra bits on page 45.)

Select the original image in your site's Files panel and duplicate it (Ctrl D in Windows, ⌘ D on the Mac). Dreamweaver automatically adds Copy of to the beginning of the duplicate's file name.

If you want to name it something else, right-click (Windows) or Ctrl-click (Mac) the item and choose Rename from the Edit drop-down menu. Once the name is highlighted, type in a new name and press Enter (Windows) or Return (Mac).

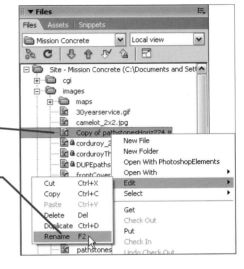

Insert the image on the page and select it by clicking on it. Make sure the Properties inspector is visible and click the Crop button in the Properties inspector. A selection area, marked by a line and darker surrounding area, appears in the middle of the image.

crop image (cont.)

Click and drag any of the black handles along the selection's edge to set your crop lines or click-and-drag in the middle to reposition the entire crop.

Double-click inside the selection and the image will be trimmed.

adjust brightness

A single button in the Properties inspector lets you adjust an image's brightness or contrast. Sometimes minor adjustments of either can really help a so-so image. You do not need to make a duplicate of the image. (See extra bits on page 45.)

On your page, click to select the image that you want to adjust.

Now click the Brightness and Contrast button in the Properties inspector.

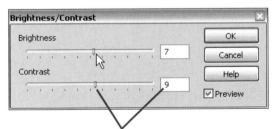

To change the brightness or contrast drag the sliders or enter new values in the adjacent text windows. (Increase the effects by sliding to the right or entering a larger number.) Click OK to apply your adjustments.

reduce image

If you have an image without lots of details, which would disappear if shrunk, you can use it to create a tiny thumbnail to add some graphic variety to a page. Detail lost from reducing and resampling cannot be recovered, so use a duplicate of your original image. (See extra bits on page 45.)

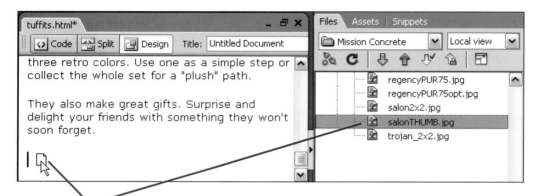

1 Make a duplicate of your original image, and drag the renamed image—in our example salon2x2.jpg is the original and salonTHUMB.jpg the renamed dupe— onto the page. The image appears on the page with small black handles at its corners.

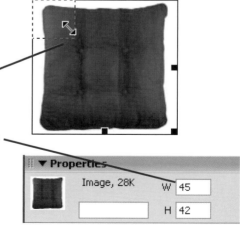

2 Press [Shift] while dragging a corner handle to reduce the image while maintaining its proportions.

Watch the pixel dimensions change in the W and H text windows in the Properties inspector to gauge how much to reduce the image.

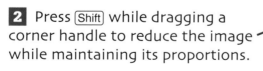

3 Release the cursor and the image appears with the new dimensions in bold—even though the actual size of the file remains the same.

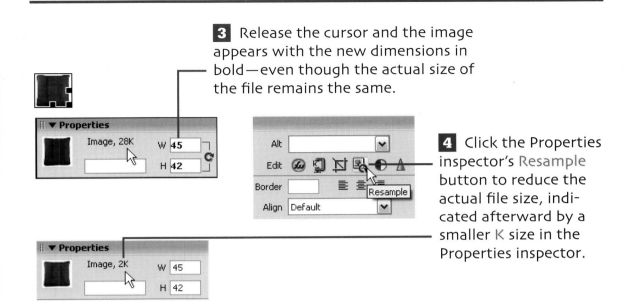

4 Click the Properties inspector's Resample button to reduce the actual file size, indicated afterward by a smaller K size in the Properties inspector.

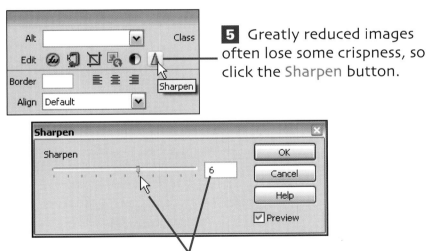

5 Greatly reduced images often lose some crispness, so click the Sharpen button.

6 Use the slider or text window in the Sharpen dialog box to adjust the amount. (Drag the slider to the right or enter a higher number in the text window to increase the sharpening.) Click OK when you're satisfied. Save the page before continuing.

add images

wrap text with images

Wrapping blocks of text around your images, instead of putting each image in its own paragraph, creates a tighter, more professional page layout. (See extra bits on page 45.)

Tuffits concrete vintage accent pillows. They look like they came right concrete, these pillows can stay outdoors year-round.

1 Click at the beginning of the text paragraph and press ←Backspace (Windows) or Delete (Mac) once to remove the paragraph break separating the image and text.

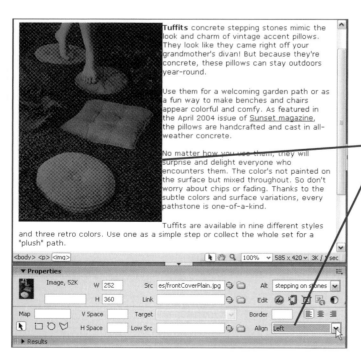

Tuffits concrete stepping stones mimic the look and charm of vintage accent pillows. They look like they came right off your grandmother's divan! But because they're concrete, these pillows can stay outdoors year-round.

Use them for a welcoming garden path or as a fun way to make benches and chairs appear colorful and comfy. As featured in the April 2004 issue of Sunset magazine, the pillows are handcrafted and cast in all-weather concrete.

No matter how you use them, they will surprise and delight everyone who encounters them. The color's not painted on the surface but mixed throughout. So don't worry about chips or fading. Thanks to the subtle colors and surface variations, every pathstone is one-of-a-kind.

Tuffits are available in nine different styles and three retro colors. Use one as a simple step or collect the whole set for a "plush" path.

`<body> <p> <img>` 100% ▾ 585 x 420 ▾ 3K / 1 sec

▼ Properties

Image, 52K   W 252   Src es/frontCoverPlain.jpg   Alt stepping on stones
              H 360   Link   Edit

Map   V Space   Target   Border
              H Space   Low Src   Align Left

▶ Results

2 Select the image and use the Align drop-down menu to choose Left. The image will be aligned on the left side of the page with the text wrapping along its right side.

add images

3 To add a little more space between the image and the surrounding text, make sure the image is selected. Now use the H Space text box to specify how many pixels of space you want between the image and text. In our example, we set the H Space to 10, which adds a moderate amount of space.

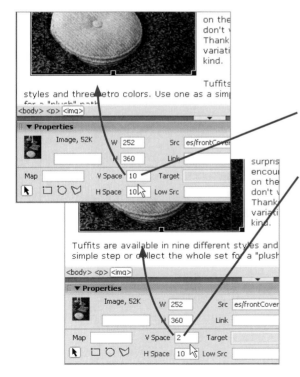

4 Use the V Space text box to set how many pixels are added above and below the image, which affects how closely the text wraps under the image. Save the page before continuing.

align text with image

The same Align drop-down menu used to wrap blocks of text around images also can be used to precisely position an image next to a single line of text. It's especially useful for pairing button-sized images with text labels.

Select an image that you've placed next to a line of text. In the Properties inspector the Align text window will be set to Default.

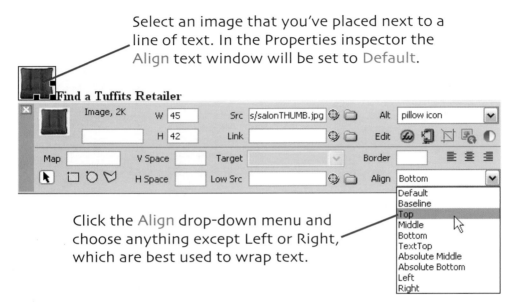

Click the Align drop-down menu and choose anything except Left or Right, which are best used to wrap text.

Release your cursor and the image realigns itself with the adjacent text.

By applying a variety of alignments before and after bits of text, you can create some surprising effects.

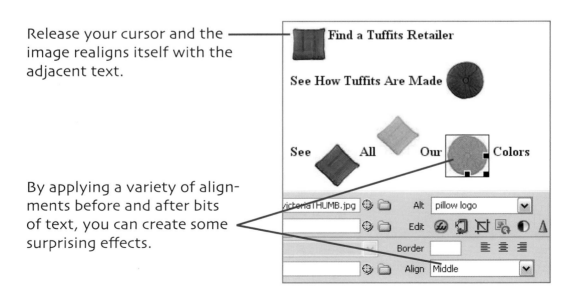

extra bits

image tools p. 34

- The blank text window right of the thumbnail is for scripts.

add image p. 35

- Keep your site's top-level folder uncluttered by creating new sub-folders when you have more than three or four related pages. Open the Files panel and right-click (Windows) or [Ctrl]-click (Mac) to reveal the New Folder choice.

- The root folder contains all your Web site's files. (In our example, it's Mission Concrete.) Save photos/graphics to the auto-generated subfolder, images, to easily find them.

- Listed below the image preview are its dimensions, file size, and estimated download time.

- Always add Alt text for your images. For dialup Web visitors, the alt text appears quickly, enabling them to skip the page if they don't want to wait for the full image. Alt text also is used by special audio Web browsers for visually impaired visitors. If the image is something like a horizontal rule, choose < empty > from the drop-down menu.

crop image p. 37

- Dreamweaver's built-in image editing only works for JPEG and GIF images, the two formats used for most photos and graphics.

adjust brightness p. 39

- The sliders can be hard to control, so type numbers in the text windows for fine adjustments.

reduce image p. 40

- You could use resampling to enlarge an image, but don't. The quality will suffer noticeably. Instead, use your regular image-editing program with the (presumably) larger original.

- When you click the Resample button, a dialog box warns you that the change is permanent. Since we're using a duplicate, click OK.

wrap text with images p. 42

- To put the image on the right side with the text down the left, choose Right in the Properties inspector's Align drop-down menu.

- The Properties inspector's H Space and V Space values are added to both sides of the image (right and left, top and bottom).

4. add tables

You are not limited to the simple approach used to build your home page in Chapter 2. Using tables to lay out a page, you can create pages more quickly and consistently. Tables also allow you to mix text, data, images, and headers, yet present it all in an easy to organize manner.

add a table

Tables can be a big help in creating simple layouts for your pages. (See extra bits on page 60.)

1 As you learned on page 10, create a new basic Web page (Ctrl N in Windows, ⌘N on the Mac) and give it a title by typing inside the Title text window.

2 Save it before continuing (Ctrl S in Windows, ⌘S on the Mac). (In our example, we titled the new page Where to Buy Tuffits and saved the file as where2buy.)

Take a moment to set several Dreamweaver options that will make using tables easier.

3 Set the Insert toolbar to Layout.

4 And click the Standard button near the center of the toolbar...

...which displays buttons for inserting tables and columns.

5 To make it easier to align your tables and cells, turn on the ruler (View > Rulers > Show), the grid (View > Grid > Show Grid), and set the grid so your drawn objects snap to it (View > Grid > Snap To Grid). Finally, set Dreamweaver so it shows how wide your tables are (View > Visual Aids > Table Widths).

add tables

6 Click inside your page, then click the Insert Table button in the Layout tool-bar. When the Table dialog box appears, use the text boxes to set the Table size and whether you want a Header, which lets you create labels for your rows or columns. In our example, we've set Rows to 1, Columns to 3, Table width to 500 pixels, Border thickness to 1 pixel, and the Header to None. Click OK to insert the new table.

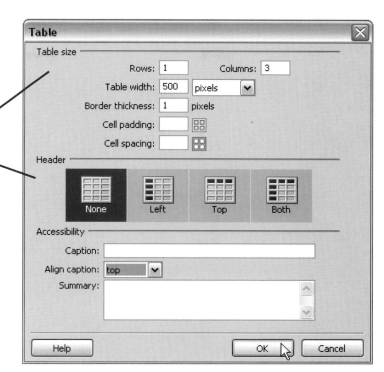

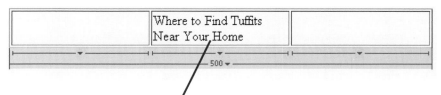

7 When the new table appears, click inside the middle cell to type a headline for the page. Don't bother formatting the text; we'll do that in Chapter 5, using style sheets. Save your work (Ctrl S in Windows, ⌘ S on the Mac).

add tables

add image to table

Tables are great for organizing large amounts of text and data, but adding a picture or two will make them more appealing. (See extra bits on page 60.)

1 Click in the first cell of the table you just created and from the Menu bar, choose Insert > Image.

2 In the Select Image Source dialog box, open your site's Images folder.

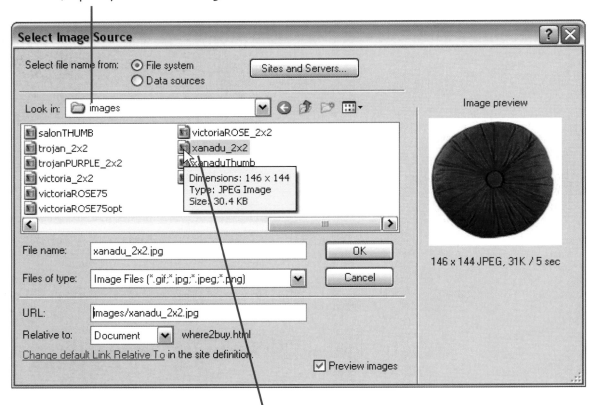

3 Choose an image, and click OK. (In our example, we chose an image of one of the Tuffits pillows.) When the Image Tab Accessibility Attributes dialog box appears, type in Alternate text for the image. (For more information, see add image on page 35.) Repeat steps 1–3 to insert another image in the far-right cell.

add tables

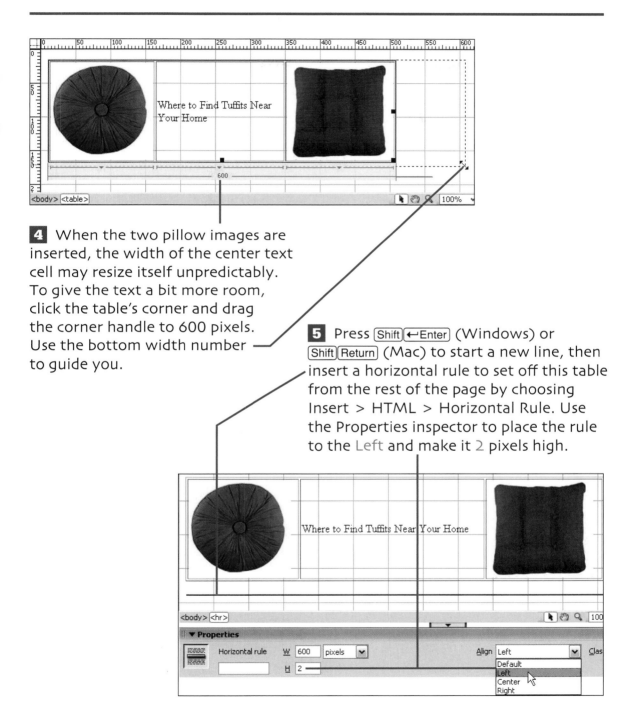

4 When the two pillow images are inserted, the width of the center text cell may resize itself unpredictably. To give the text a bit more room, click the table's corner and drag the corner handle to 600 pixels. Use the bottom width number to guide you.

5 Press Shift←Enter (Windows) or Shift Return (Mac) to start a new line, then insert a horizontal rule to set off this table from the rest of the page by choosing Insert > HTML > Horizontal Rule. Use the Properties inspector to place the rule to the Left and make it 2 pixels high.

add tables

add labels

Dreamweaver automatically formats row and column labels as centered and bold. That makes the labels, also known as table headers, easy to scan for anyone viewing the table. (See extra bits on page 60.)

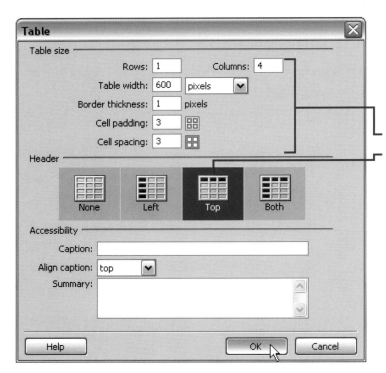

Press ⌈Enter⌉ (Windows) or ⌈Return⌉ (Mac) to start a new line below the first table and rule bar, then insert a new table and use the Table dialog box to set the Table size, and create a Header with labels across the Top.

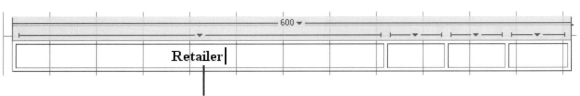

When the new table appears on the page, click in the header's far-left cell and type in a label. Add labels for the rest of the headers, pressing ⌈Tab⌉ to move from cell to cell. (In our example, we use Retailer, Address, City, and Zip, which match the tabular data we'll soon import.)

add tables

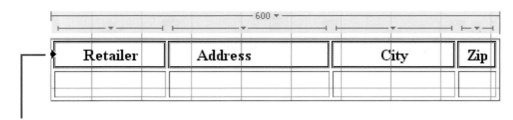

Once you've added all your labels, click in any of the cells, then click the Insert Row Above button in the Layout toolbar.

A blank four-cell row appears right above the labeled row. Select the new row by clicking and dragging your cursor across all four cells, which will be highlighted.

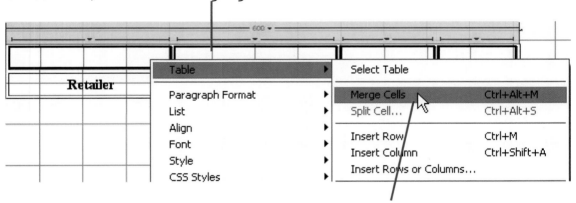

Right-click (Ctrl-click on the Mac), and choose Table > Merge Cells from the drop-down menu.

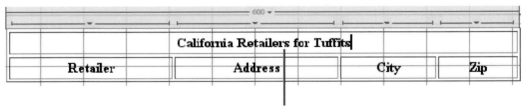

Click inside the now-merged cell and type California Retailers for Tuffits, which retains the default centered and bold formatting of the items in the original table header row (Retailer–Zip).

add tables

import tabular data

Nothing beats a table for clearly presenting spreadsheet data or tab-separated text imported from a word-processing document. (See extra bits on page 60.)

1 Press (Enter) (Windows) or (Return) (Mac) to start a new paragraph just below the table you've already created.

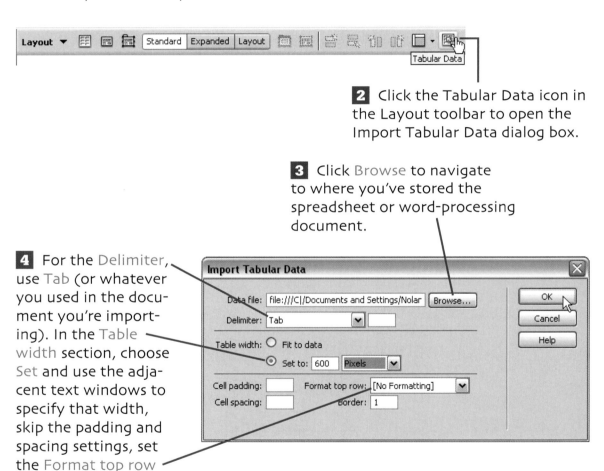

2 Click the Tabular Data icon in the Layout toolbar to open the Import Tabular Data dialog box.

3 Click Browse to navigate to where you've stored the spreadsheet or word-processing document.

4 For the Delimiter, use Tab (or whatever you used in the document you're importing). In the Table width section, choose Set and use the adjacent text windows to specify that width, skip the padding and spacing settings, set the Format top row to [No Formatting] and click OK.

California Retailers for Tuffits			
Retailer	**Address**	**City**	**Zip**
		600 ▾	
Agorra Bidg Supply	5965 Dougherty Road	Dublin	94568
Clark's Home and Garden	23040 Clawiter Rd.	Hayward	94545
Christv Vault Co.	44100 Christy St.	Fremont	94538
Diamond K Supply	3671 Mt.Diablo Blvd.	Lafayette	94549
L.H.Voss	2445 Vista Del Monte.Concord	94520	
Morgan's Masonry	P.O. Box 127	San Ramon	94583

5 The data appears on the Web page arranged in its own table. Save the page (Ctrl S in Windows, ⌘ S on the Mac).

6 Click and drag your cursor until you select all the cells in the second table, then copy them (press Ctrl C in Windows, ⌘ C on the Mac).

		600 ▾		
Agorra Bidg Supply	5965 Dougherty Road		Dublin	94568
Clark's Home and Garden	23040 Clawiter Rd.		Hayward	94545
Christv Vault Co.	44100 Christy St.		Fremont	94538
Diamond K Supply	3671 Mt.Diablo Blvd.		Lafayette	94549
L.H.Voss	2445 Vista Del Monte.Concord		94520	
Morgan's Masonry	P.O. Box 127		San Ramon	94583
Morgan Bros. Patio	14305 Washington Ave.		San Leandro	94578
Orco Const. Supply	P.O. Box5058		Livermore	94550
Regan Nursery.Inc.	4268 Decoto Rd.		Fremont	94555
Air-Vol	P.O.Box 931		San Luis Obispo93406	

7 Click in the first cell in the blank row of the top table and paste your selection there (press Ctrl V in Windows, ⌘ V on the Mac). The copied cells will appear in the first table with their cell formatting intact. Having moved the second table's contents to the first table, select the second table and delete it.

California Retailers for Tuffits			
Retailer	**Address**	**City**	**Zip**
Agorra Bidg Supply	5965 Dougherty Road	Dublin	94568
Clark's Home and Garden	23040 Clawiter Rd.	Hayward	94545
Christv Vault Co.	44100 Christy St.	Fremont	94538
Diamond K Supply	3671 Mt.Diablo Blvd.	Lafayette	94549
L.H.Voss	2445 Vista Del Monte.Concord	94520	
Morgan's Masonry	P.O. Box 127	San Ramon	94583
Morgan Bros. Patio	14305 Washington Ave.	San Leandro	94578
Orco Const. Supply	P.O. Box5058	Livermore	94550

add tables

edit table

Inevitably, our example table has a few errors. Several blank cells appear because the imported data mistakenly had an extra tab character between several retailers' names and addresses. Dreamweaver makes it easy to fix the problem.

1 You cannot directly delete a blank cell in a table because of the table's interlocking grid of rows and columns. But you can move data from several cells and delete the blank row created by the shift. (In our example, we select the cell with the street address for one of the retailers.)

Broadmoor Lumber Co.		1350 El Camino Real	S.S.F.
94080			

Broadmoor Lumber Co.	1350 El Camino Real		S.S.F.
~~94080~~			

Broadmoor Lumber Co.	1350 El Camino Real	S.S.F.	94080

2 Click and drag to select the text, then drag the highlighted text from one cell to the other.

3 Repeat for the misplaced city and zip code data, which leaves you a blank row that you can select and delete.

add tables

format table colors

To make it easier for your Web visitors to read the information in long tables, we'll apply some color formatting. (See extra bits on page 60.)

Select the entire table and choose Commands > Format Table to open the Format Table dialog box, which includes more than a dozen preset table color combinations.

Use the various drop-down menus to pick your colors and how often the colors of the rows alternate.

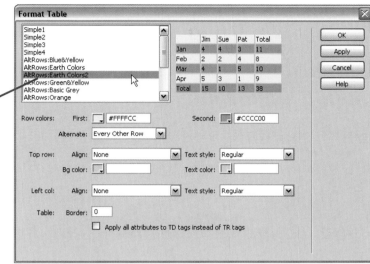

In our example, we've changed the First and Second row colors to echo the page's pillow colors and set Alternate to Every Two Rows for a less busy look.

Click Apply to preview your choices and click OK to close the dialog box. Be sure to save the page when you're done.

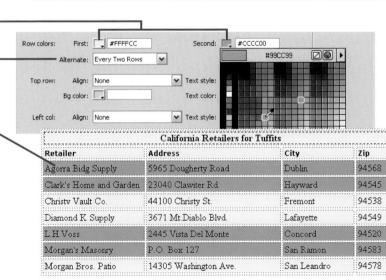

sort tables

Dreamweaver can automatically sort tabular data by column—a neat trick that lets you tinker with how the data is organized long after you've imported it into your table. There's just one catch: tables cannot be sorted if they include a cell that spans multiple columns. We've got just such a cell in our example, but we can do a quick cut and paste to work around this restriction. (See extra bits on page 60.)

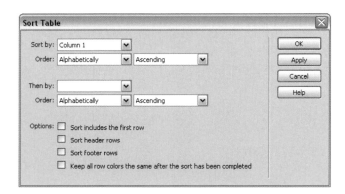

Select the column-spanning cell (in our example, it's California Retailers for Tuffits) and cut it from the page ([Ctrl][X] in Windows, [⌘][X] on the Mac). Now select the table and choose Commands > Sort Table to open the Sort Table dialog box.

Use the Sort by drop-down menu to choose which column will control the sort, then use the Order drop-down menu to set whether the sort is done Alphabetically (or Numerically) and whether it's Ascending (or Descending) order. In our example, we sort by Column 3 (City) because that is the easiest way for site visitors to find a nearby store. We also set Then by to sort using Column 4 (Zip), which helps big-city residents. Click Apply to preview the sort and click OK to close the dialog box.

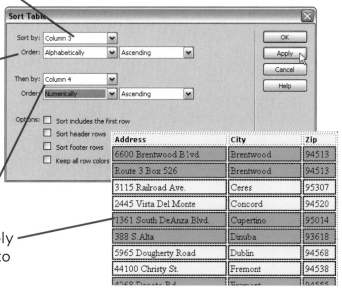

Once the sort's done, insert a row above the header row, merge those new cells into one and paste in your original header. (In our example, it's California Retailers for Tuffits.) Be sure to save the page and you're done.

California Retailers for Tuffits			
Retailer	**Address**	**City**	**Zip**
Big B Lumber	6600 Brentwood Blvd.	Brentwood	94513
Norman's Brentwood Nursery	Route 3 Box 526	Brentwood	94513
Masonry Systems	3115 Railroad Ave.	Ceres	95307

add tables

extra bits

add a table p. 48

- Use the Table dialog box's Accessibility section to create an explanatory Caption that will be read aloud by special audio Web browsers for visually impaired visitors. If needed, add details in the Summary field.

add image to table p. 50

- If you're having trouble selecting a table, click near the table and then press Ctrl A in Windows or ⌘ A on the Mac. Or click the <table> tag down in the status bar.

- For more precision in resizing the table, type a number into the W field of the Properties inspector and press Tab.

add labels p. 52

- The Table dialog box Header options—None, Left, Top, and Both—let you skip adding labels, label only the rows, label only the columns, or label both rows and columns.

import tabular data p. 54

- Before importing, use your spreadsheet or word-processing program to save the data in comma- or tab-delimited form.

- Sometimes the Set drop-down menu in the Table Width section of the Import Tabular Data dialog box will switch to Percent—even if you previously set it to Pixels. So double-check before clicking OK.

- Our copy-and-paste example works because each table had the same number of columns. You cannot, for example, copy 6 columns and paste them into 4 columns.

format table colors p. 57

- By using Ctrl-click in Windows or ⌘-click on the Mac, you also can select non-adjacent columns or cells. Then you can format all the selections at once.

sort tables p. 58

- By default, the Options in the Sort Table dialog box are not checked, since you seldom want the header or footer rows sorted.

5. use style sheets

Style sheets, also known as external style sheets or Cascading Style Sheets (CSS), are tremendous time savers when formatting pages. You can create sets of styles that are easy to combine and recombine as needed. In this chapter, we'll create several style sheets and use them to replace our home page's internal styles. We'll then create some additional styles within the main style sheet that can be applied to any page in the Web site.

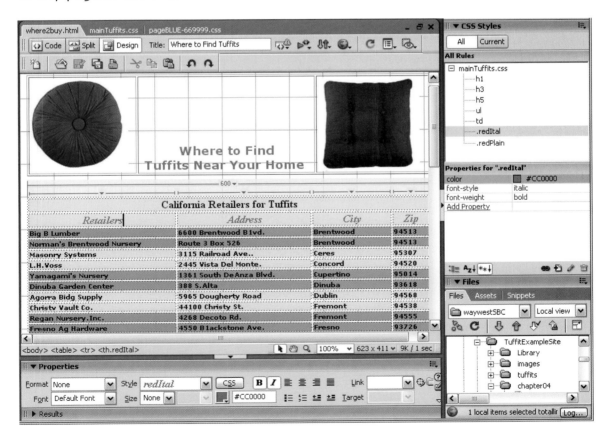

create style sheet

Though we set colors and sorted a table in Chapter 4, we did not format any of its text because all that tweaking—setting fonts, sizes, and styles—would only apply to that page. Instead we're going to use the heading styles we created on pages 22–30 as the foundation of an external style sheet. Once it's created, that external style sheet helps you quickly format other pages, including the table page. (See extra bits on page 74.)

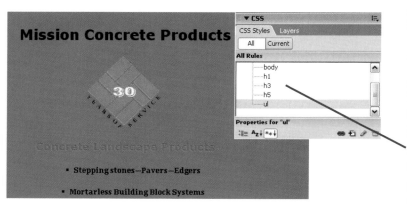

1 Open your home page (in our Mission Concrete Products example, Chapter 2's place-holder image has been replaced with the actual logo). Open the CSS Styles tab (Window > CSS Styles), which lists all the style rules created for the page.

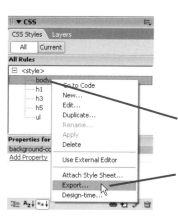

2 Since we don't want all our pages to be blue like the example home page, we'll create separate style sheets for the page color and for the headings. In the CSS Styles tab, right-click (Windows) or Ctrl-click (Mac) body, which controls the page background, and choose Export from the drop-down menu.

3 In the dialog box that appears, navigate to the folder where the target index page is stored (in our example tuffits).

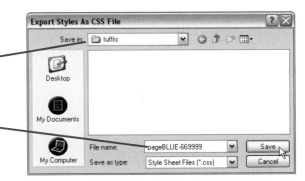

4 Give it a distinct file name (pageBLUE-669999 isn't poetry but it's clear), and click Save to close the dialog box.

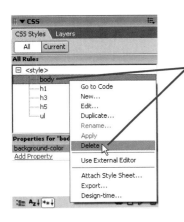

5 Having exported the body rule, right-click (Windows) or Ctrl-click (Mac) body and choose Delete from the drop-down menu.

6 Because you're deleting the rule controlling background color, the home page turns white and the body rule disappears from the CSS Styles tab. (We'll restore the color on page 66 by attaching our external style sheet to the page.)

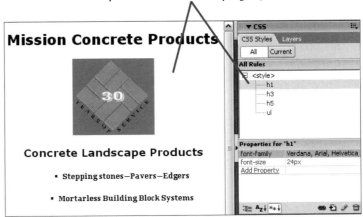

create style sheet (cont.)

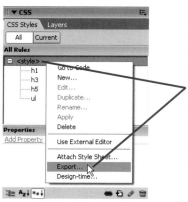

7 We can use everything remaining in the style rule in our main external style sheet. Right-click (Windows) or ⌃Ctrl-click (Mac) < style > and choose Export from the drop-down menu to create an external style sheet based on this internal style.

8 In the dialog box that appears, navigate to where you stored the body style sheet, and name it based on the site's name. Click Save to close the dialog box. Before going to the next page, from the Menu bar, choose File > Save All.

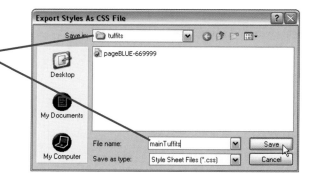

attach style sheets

Having exported the home page's styles to the safety of the external style sheet, we now can delete its internal styles and attach two external style sheets to control its appearance. (See extra bits on page 74.)

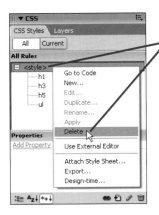

1 With the home page still open, right-click (Windows) or Ctrl-click (Mac) the < style > rule remaining in the CSS Styles tab and choose Delete from the drop-down menu.

2 The page's CSS Styles tab now shows (no styles defined), so click the Attach Style Sheet button.

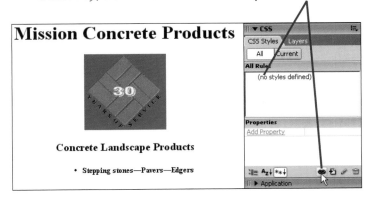

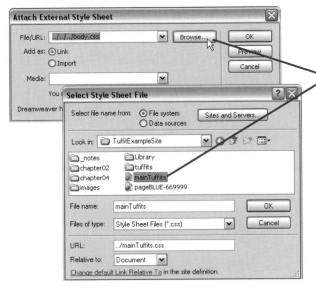

3 In the Attach External Style Sheet dialog box, click Browse to navigate to the external style sheet you created on the previous page (mainTuffits in our example).

4 Click OK to close the Select Style Sheet dialog box. When the Attach External Style Sheet dialog box reappears, click OK again to return to the home page.

attach style sheets (cont.)

5 The home page's CSS Styles tab now links it to the external style sheet (mainTuffits.css) and all its style rules.

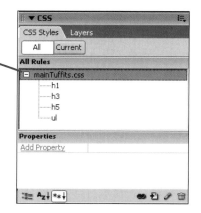

6 We still need to restore the home page's background color. Click the Attach Style Sheet button again and repeat step 3 to attach the pageBLUE-669999 style sheet. Once you close the Attach External Style Sheet dialog box, the page appears just as it did originally. The difference is that its appearance now is controlled by the two external style sheets, which you can edit any time to change the home page—and any other pages linked to them.

7 Before going to the next page, choose File > Save All, then close the home page.

use style sheets

apply external styles

Once you attach style sheets to a page, you select items on the page and apply those styles. (See extra bits on page 74.)

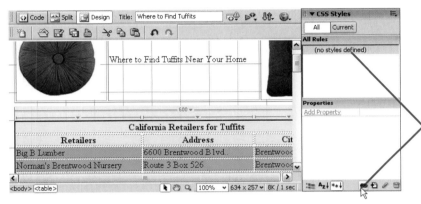

1 If it's no longer open, reopen the table page you created in Chapter 4 (where2buy.html in our example). While we formatted and sorted the table, the page contains no styles, so click the CSS Styles tab's Attach Style Sheet button.

2 In the Attach External Style Sheet dialog box, the external style sheet you created earlier is listed automatically (mainTuffits in our example). Click OK to close the dialog box.

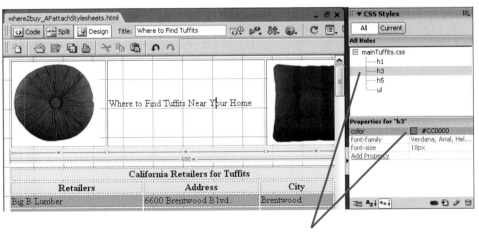

3 The table page's CSS Styles tab now shows that it's linked to the external style sheet (mainTuffits.css) and all the rules within it, such as h3.

apply external styles (cont.)

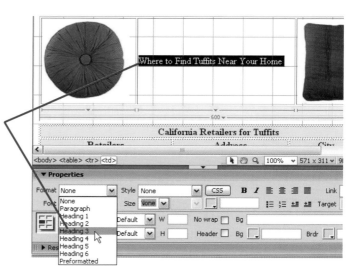

4 Select the center text in the top table, and choose Heading 3 from the Format drop-down menu.

5 Press [Tab] and the text immediately assumes all the properties assigned in the external style sheet's h3 rule, including the font and color.

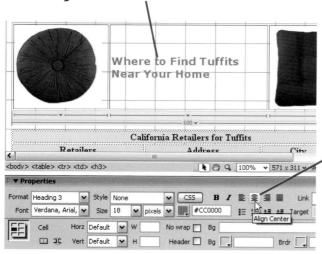

6 Click anywhere in the heading and click the Align Center button in the Properties inspector. The centering is applied only to this page, without changing any h3 properties in the external style sheet.

7 From the Menu bar, choose File > Save All before going to the next page.

use style sheets

add to style sheet

Because CSS control was so awkward in earlier versions of Dreamweaver, it was common practice to use the Properties inspector to style single HTML tags within every page you built. That approach promoted spontaneity, but it also tended to generate a sprawl of unrelated single-page styles. If, instead, you use the CSS Styles tab, you can create a more powerful site-wide system. Now that we've attached style sheets to our pages, it's easy to add more CSS rules that can be used on any page.

1 If it's no longer open, reopen the table page (where2buy.html in our example). Make sure the Properties inspector and CSS Styles tab are visible.

2 Click in any cell of the tabular data you imported on page 54.

3 The <td> tag is highlighted in the status bar because that tag controls cell contents.

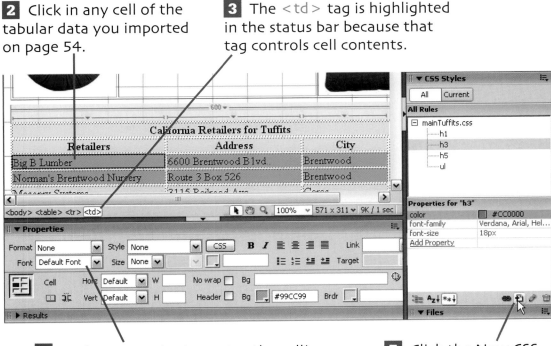

4 In the Properties inspector the cell's text has not been formatted—just the background color (#99CC99 in our example).

5 Click the New CSS Rule button to create a new rule for cell content.

add to style sheet (cont.)

6 In the New CSS Rule dialog box, Tag is already selected and the Tag field is set to td. The Define in field already says mainTuffits.css since you're adding a new rule to that external style sheet. Click OK to close the dialog box.

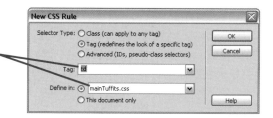

7 In the CSS Rule Definition dialog box, click the Font drop-down menu and choose one of the six font groups.

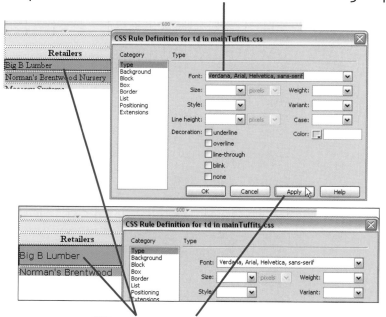

8 Click Apply to see how the text changes from its default serif setting within your table. To try another font group, make another selection in the Font drop-down menu and click Apply again.

9 Once you find a satisfactory grouping, select Block in the dialog box's left-hand column and use the drop-down menus to set Vertical alignment to baseline and Text align to left. Click OK to close the dialog box.

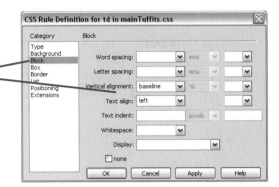

10 The table's text reflects your changes.

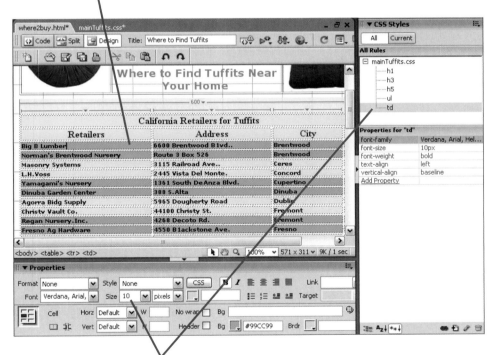

11 The changes also appear in the CSS Styles tab and Properties inspector. Any page containing cell text automatically displays these properties when linked (attached) to this external style sheet.

create custom rule

Creating custom CSS rules (also called class styles) gives your style sheets a modular quality. Instead of simply adding fixed styles to your set of external style sheets—as you did with the cell content in the previous section—you can customize them as needed. That's because custom rules, such as the redItal rule we create below, can be applied to any tag, like that cell text, and still preserve the original tag's font and size properties. The biggest advantage: creative flexibility without stylistic chaos. (See extra bits on page 74.)

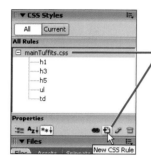

1 Open any page to which you've already attached your main css style sheet (mainTuffits.css in our example). In the CSS Styles tab, make sure the style sheet is selected and click the New CSS Rule button.

2 Choose Class, type in a descriptive name (redItal in our example) and use the Define in drop-down menu to choose your main style sheet (mainTuffits.css). Click OK to close the dialog box.

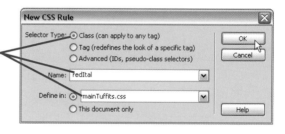

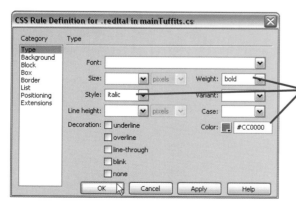

3 In the CSS Rule Definition dialog box, use the drop-down menus to set the Weight to bold, the Style to italic, and the Color to #CC0000 (red). Click OK to close the dialog box.

use style sheets

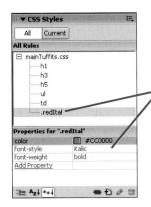

4 The new rule appears in the CSS Styles tab with the properties you assigned in the previous step.

5 To apply the new custom rule, select some text in any page attached to that external style sheet.

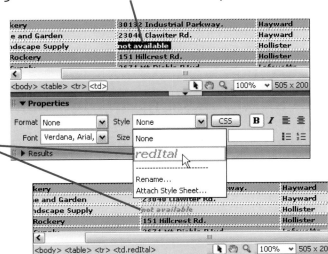

6 Click the Style drop-down menu, choose the new style (redItal), and it will be applied to the text—without wiping out any of its other properties.

7 Before quitting Dreamweaver, choose File > Save All.

extra bits

create style sheet p. 62

- While you can take it too far, in general try to break your formatting into smaller components. That way you can, for example, apply the heading styles to every page without also making them all blue.

- It's common to simply name a site-wide style sheet main.css. But since you may eventually create multiple sites, make it a habit to include the site's name, such as mainTuffits.css, to avoid the confusion of having multiple main.css files.

attach style sheets p. 65

- In the CSS Styles tab, instead of right-clicking (Windows) or Ctrl-clicking (Mac) the style rules, you also can use the buttons at the lower right: ⊞ to attach a style sheet, ⊞ to create a new rule, ✎ to edit a style sheet, and ⊞ to delete anything.

apply external styles p. 67

- If you think a particular style might be useful on many pages, work within the external style sheet. If, as in the example of centering Heading 3, you do not want to apply that particular style site-wide, use the Properties inspector to apply it to a single page.

create custom rule p. 72

- Officially when naming a custom rule in the New CSS Rule dialog box, you're supposed to start it with a period, for example .redItal. In practice, however, as long as you also select Class, Dreamweaver (Windows or Mac) automatically adds the period after you close the dialog box.

- That same custom rule then can be used to apply red italic to any of your other styles.

use style sheets

6. create links

The Web's magic comes largely from the hyperlink, which lets Web users jump from page to image to email to almost anywhere on the Internet. Links fall into two categories: internal links, which connect different items within your own Web site, and external links, which connect to items out on the larger Web. Before we begin linking some of the pages created in previous chapters, switch the Insert toolbar to Common, which includes link-related buttons.

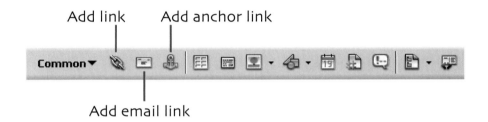

Add link   Add anchor link

Add email link

link text internally

Dreamweaver makes creating links between pages on your Web site a point-and-click affair. (See extra bits on page 88.)

1 Open your home page and select text you want to link to another page on your Web site. (In our example, we are linking text on the Mission Concrete Products home page to the Tuffits products page.)

2 Make sure the Files panel and the Properties inspector are both visible.

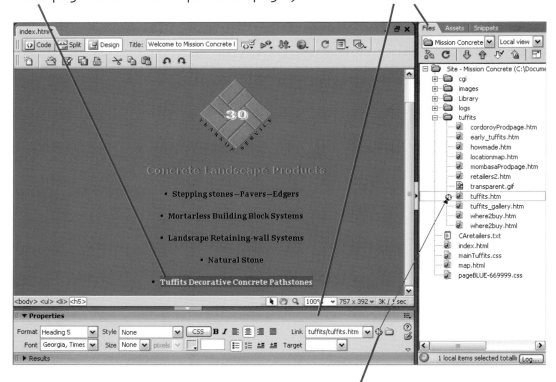

3 Click the compass-like Point to File icon and drag the line that appears to your to-be-linked file in the Files panel. Release your cursor and the file path to that file appears in the Link text window.

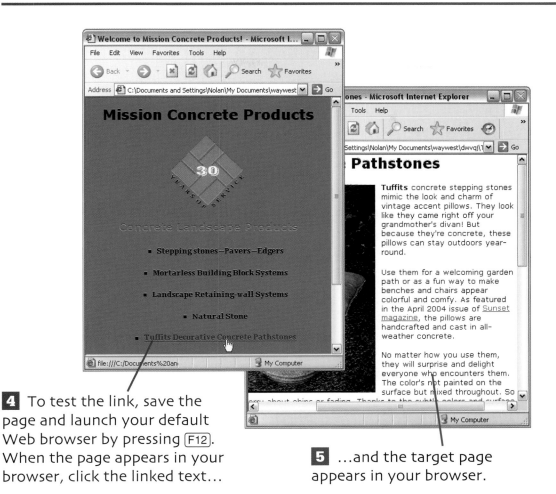

4 To test the link, save the page and launch your default Web browser by pressing F12. When the page appears in your browser, click the linked text...

5 ...and the target page appears in your browser.

link text externally

Links to items that are not part of your own Web site are called external links. While we use text in this example, you can create external links using images as well. (See extra bits on page 88.)

1 Make sure the Properties inspector is visible, then select the text you want to link to a page out on the Web.

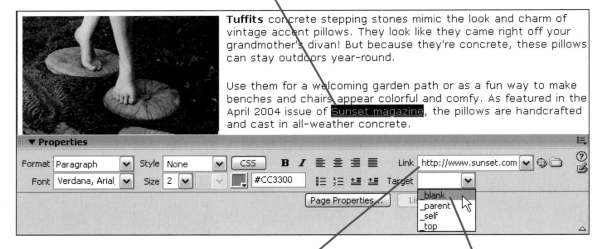

2 Type the full Web address for the outside page, including the http://, directly into the Link text window...

3 ...then select _blank from the Target drop-down menu. Save the page and test the link in your browser, where the outside link will open in a new window.

color site links

By default, unvisited Web links are blue and underlined while visited links are purple and underlined. Dreamweaver, however, makes it easy to change the color and style of all your links to match your Web site's overall look. Here we'll set colors for all four link states: unvisited link, visited, hover, and active. (See extra bits on page 88.)

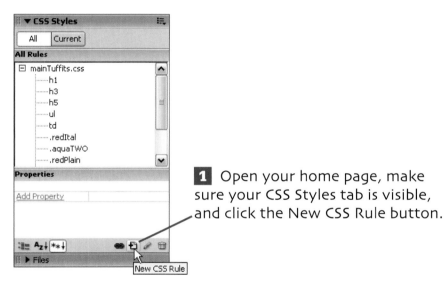

1 Open your home page, make sure your CSS Styles tab is visible, and click the New CSS Rule button.

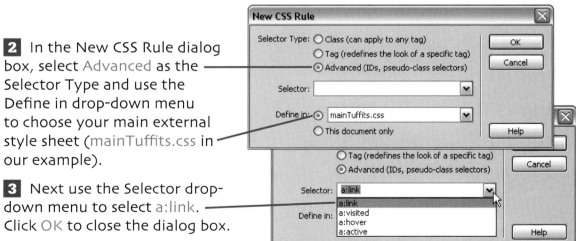

2 In the New CSS Rule dialog box, select Advanced as the Selector Type and use the Define in drop-down menu to choose your main external style sheet (mainTuffits.css in our example).

3 Next use the Selector drop-down menu to select a:link. Click OK to close the dialog box.

color site links (cont.)

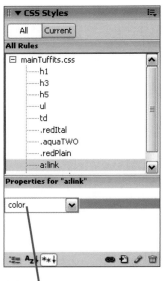

4 We don't need to use the CSS Rule Definition dialog box, so when it appears click OK to close it.

5 When the new a:link rule appears in the CSS Styles tab, click the Add Property button in the Properties pane.

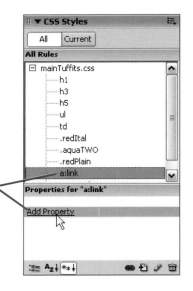

6 Type color into the text field that appears and press Tab.

create links

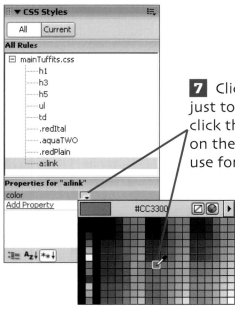

7 Click the small box that appears just to the right of the color field and click the eye-dropper-shaped cursor on the box for the color you want to use for this link state.

8 The color with its number code will be added to the list of properties for the a:link.

9 Click the New CSS Rule button again to add another link state.

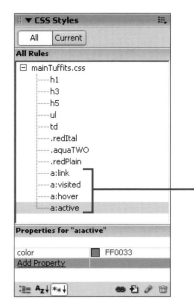

10 Repeat steps 2–9 to create and define rules for the remaining three link states: visited, hover, and active. When you're done, all four will be listed in your main external style sheet.

11 To apply these link colors to any page on your site, just attach this external style sheet, as explained on page 65.

create links 81

add email link

By embedding addresses in your email links, you make it easy for readers to send email to you and others listed on your Web site.

1 Select the text on your page that you want to link to email. (In our example, we've selected Contact us! from a bit of text added to the Mission Concrete home page.)

2 Click the Email button on the Insert toolbar.

3 The selected text appears in the top field in the Email Link dialog box. Type the email address into the bottom field and click OK.

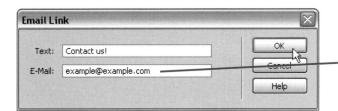

4 The text selected on your page becomes a link. Test it by saving the page, opening it in your Web browser, and clicking the link. Your default email program automatically creates a new message addressed to the email address on the Web page.

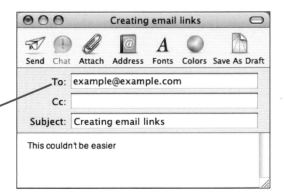

add anchor link

Anchor links enable Web visitors to jump to a specific spot within a long Web page, sparing readers from scrolling through it. You must first create an anchor to mark the particular spot in the target document. Then you create a link to that spot. (See extra bits on page 88.)

1 Open a Web page and click on the particular spot where you want to add an anchor link. (In our example, we're marking the start of our Northern California retailers.)

2 Click the Named Anchor button in the Insert toolbar.

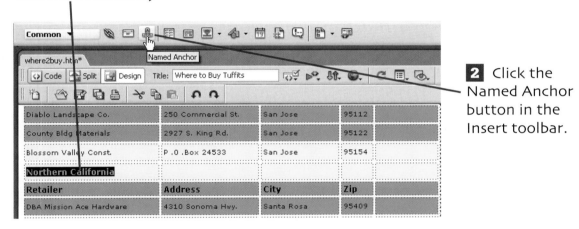

3 Type a distinctive name in the Named Anchor dialog box and click OK.

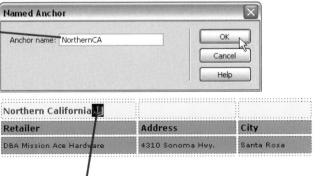

4 An anchor icon will be added next to the selected text. Save the page, which also saves the anchor name.

add anchor link (cont.)

5 Now select the text you want linked to the anchor.

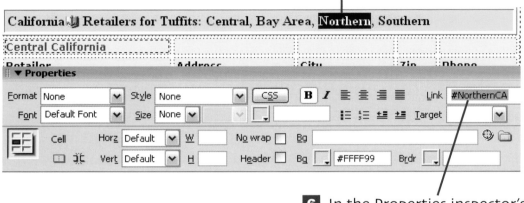

6 In the Properties inspector's Link text window, type # and (with no space between) the exact anchor name you created in step 3 (#NorthernCA in our example.) Press [Enter] (Windows) or [Return] (Mac) to activate the link.

create links

link image

Images are easy to spot on a page and easy to click, so don't limit yourself to creating just text links. Creating internal and external links with images works exactly as it does for text links.

With the Files panel and Properties inspector both visible, open the page containing the image you want to link to something, and select it.

Use the Point to File icon to draw a line to the file to which you want to link the image. (In our example, we are linking a button-sized image to our list of Tuffits retailers.)

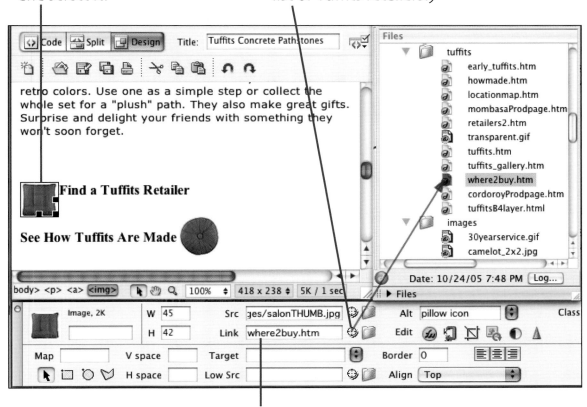

The file path for the other file appears in the Link text window. Release your cursor to create the link.

create image map

Image maps take the basic idea behind an image link and give it extra power by making it possible to link separate hot spots within the image to multiple files. It saves space on the page and provides an elegant, easy-to-understand interface for your site. (See extra bits on page 88.)

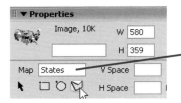

1 With the Properties inspector visible, open the image for which you want to create an image map. Type a name for the image map in the Map text window.

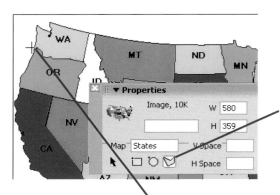

2 Based on the shape of the hot spot you'll be creating, click one of the three shape buttons. (In our example, we've chosen the freeform polygon to create an Oregon-shaped hot spot.)

3 Click in your image where you want to begin creating the hot spot, which will be marked by a cross-hair.

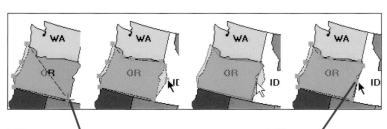

4 Build your hot spot one click at a time along the boundary of the underlying image.

5 If you need to adjust the hot spot's boundary, click any square-shaped handle and drag it to a new spot.

create links

6 After building your hot spots, select one and use the Properties inspector's Point to File icon to link it to a document. (In our example, we've linked to an anchor within the file.)

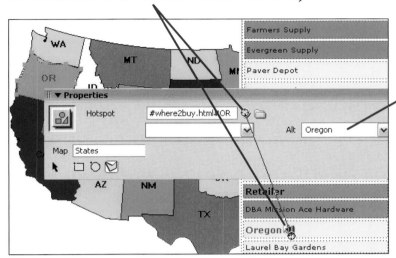

7 Be sure to add an Alt name for the hot spot to help you keep it straight. Repeat these steps for each hot spot you've created, giving each its own Alt name.

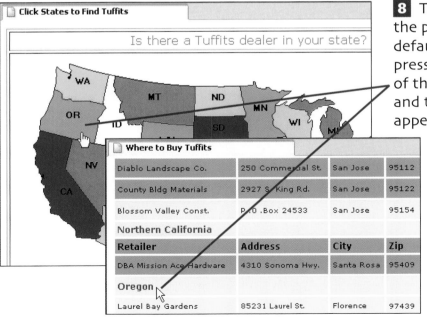

8 To test the link, save the page, and launch your default Web browser by pressing F12. Click any of the image's hot spots and the linked page appears in your browser.

create links

extra bits

link text internally p. 76

- If the file to which you're linking is not already part of your Web site, click the Folder icon next to the Link drop-down menu and navigate to it. When Dreamweaver asks to import the file into the site, click Yes.

link text externally p. 78

- Selecting _blank from the Target drop-down menu opens a new window in the visitor's browser— ensuring that your site remains visible as the visitor looks at the external Web page.

color site links p. 79

- Because we only want to color our four link styles, we skip the CSS Rule Definition dialog box. But feel free to experiment. The Block category, for example, lets you create a navigation bar of colored boxes.

- You also could create the links as their own separate style sheet. The drawback is you have to attach it to all your pages. By creating the link styles within the main style sheet, that's one less style sheet to attach.

add anchor link p. 83

- The anchor doesn't need to be tied to a text selection.

- Dreamweaver inserts an icon next to your anchor-link text just to help you spot it. It will not be visible on your Web site. To turn these icons off or on, choose View > Visual Aids > Invisible Elements.

create image map p. 86

- Image map names should not include any blank spaces or special characters.

- The hot spot need not exactly match the underlying shape. Just cover the portion your visitors will most likely click.

- If you can't arrange your document windows to point directly to an anchor, use Browse to reach the file. At the end of the file name selected in the Link text window, type a # and the exact name of the anchor (without a space).

- A hot spot can link to an internal or external file.

7. reuse items to save time

Think of the Assets tab as Dreamweaver's grand central timesaver. It automatically lists which images, color swatches, and external links you use on your site. If you want to use those items again, the Assets tab makes it easy to quickly find what you need. The Assets tab also includes two other major timesavers— library items and templates, both of which we'll use in our project.

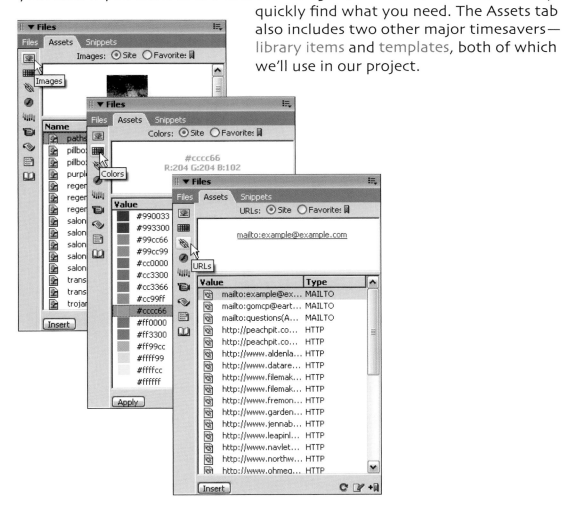

create a favorite

By creating favorites from the lists generated by the Assets tab, you always have your most-used items handy.

1 Press F11 to open the Assets tab and make sure the Site radio button is selected.

2 Select the category button you need in the left-hand column. (In our example, we've chosen the Images button because with so many images used, creating a shorter favorites list is essential.)

3 Select the image file you want to mark as a favorite.

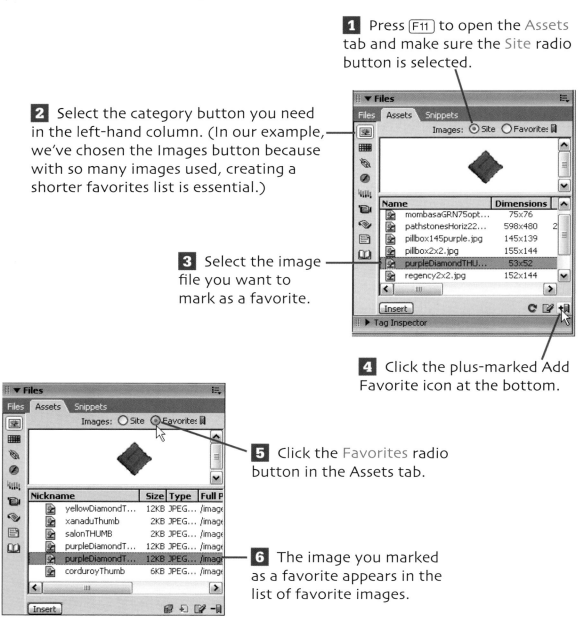

4 Click the plus-marked Add Favorite icon at the bottom.

5 Click the Favorites radio button in the Assets tab.

6 The image you marked as a favorite appears in the list of favorite images.

reuse items to save time

create a library item

Make library items of anything you use repeatedly. It can be something simple like a 2 x 400-pixel rule. Or it can be as elaborate as an entire table containing images and links. Short or long, the real benefit of a library item comes when you need to make a change—change it once and all pages using it automatically update. (See extra bits on page 105.)

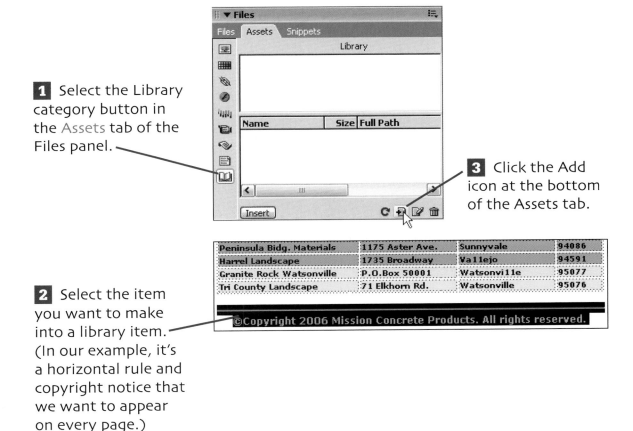

1 Select the Library category button in the Assets tab of the Files panel.

3 Click the Add icon at the bottom of the Assets tab.

2 Select the item you want to make into a library item. (In our example, it's a horizontal rule and copyright notice that we want to appear on every page.)

create a library item (cont.)

4 Click OK when Dreamweaver warns that the library item cannot include the styling from the original page.

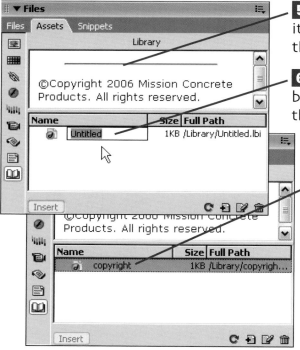

5 A preview of the new library item appears in the top half of the Assets tab.

6 The still untitled file will be selected automatically in the bottom half of the tab.

7 Give the new library item a distinctive name and press ⌷Tab⌷ to apply it.

reuse items to save time

edit library item

In our example, we mistakenly left out a space in our copyright notice.

To fix it, we'll click the Edit icon at the bottom of the Assets tab.

When the library item appears, make your correction.

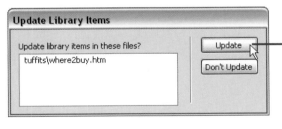

Save the changes and when Dreamweaver asks if it should change any pages containing this library item, click Update.

When a dialog box appears listing which pages were updated, click Close. The Asset tab's preview of the library item updates to reflect the changes. Close the edited library page to get it out of your way.

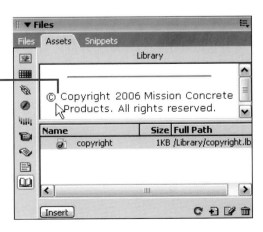

reuse items to save time

insert library item

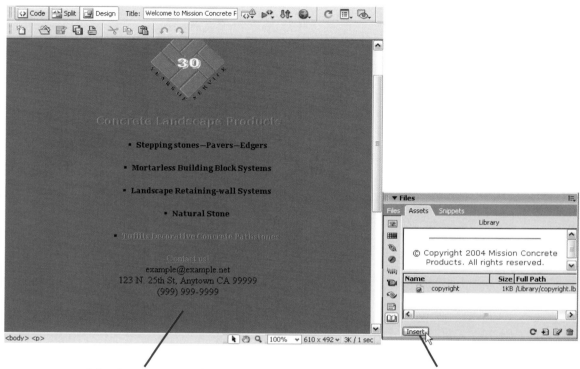

With the Assets tab of the Files panel open and visible, click in the open page where you want to place the selected library item...

...and then click the Asset tab's Insert button.

reuse items to save time

The item appears in the page without any styling.
A light yellow background and a nearby yellow
icon indicate that it's a library item.

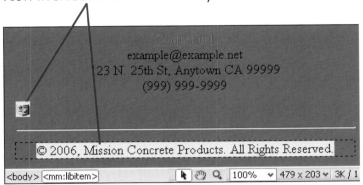

When you save the page and view it within
a Web browser, however, this yellow marker
will not be visible.

create a template

Templates are great timesavers for building pages with an identical layout but variable content. In our example, we've created a Tuffits product template, which can then be used to generate pages for each product. Templates require that you mark which parts can be changed in the individual pages created from it. (See extra bits on page 105.)

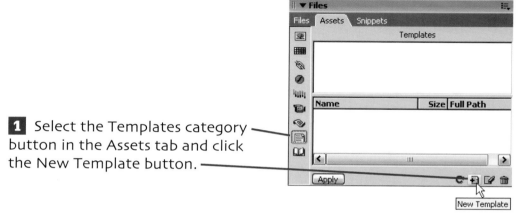

1 Select the Templates category button in the Assets tab and click the New Template button.

2 The still untitled file will be selected automatically in the bottom half of the tab. Give the new template item a distinctive name and press ⎄Tab⎄ to apply it. (In our example, we've named it product since we'll be using it as the template for all Tuffits products.)

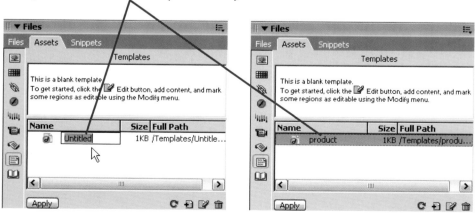

reuse items to save time

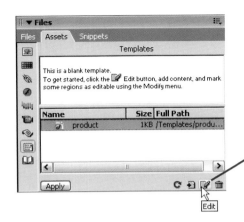

3 With the template still selected, click the Edit button at the bottom of the Assets tab.

4 The new—and entirely blank—template page opens.

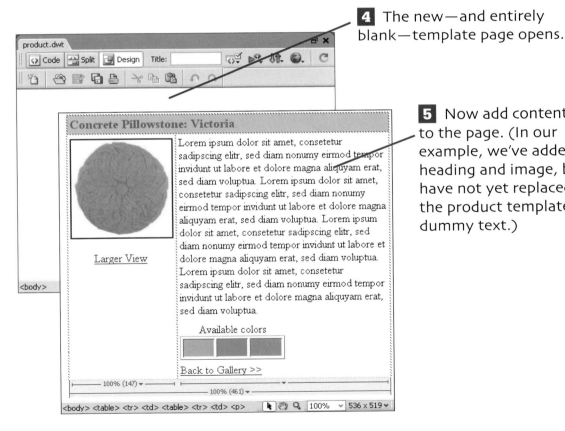

5 Now add content to the page. (In our example, we've added a heading and image, but have not yet replaced the product template's dummy text.)

reuse items to save time

create a template (cont.)

6 Once you finish adding your content, you need to mark which items in the template can be changed or edited. Make sure the Insert toolbar is set to Common, then select a page item (in our example, the main text block).

7 Click the Templates button in the toolbar and choose Editable Region in the drop-down menu.

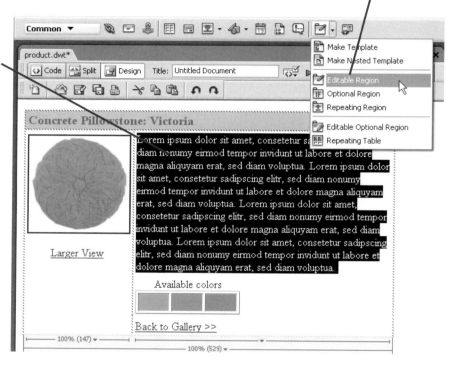

8 When the New Editable Region dialog box appears, select the generic name in the Name text window, type in a more descriptive name, and click OK.

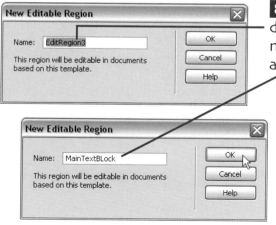

reuse items to save time

9 Your region name will be added to the template page.

10 Continue adding and naming editable regions until you're done.

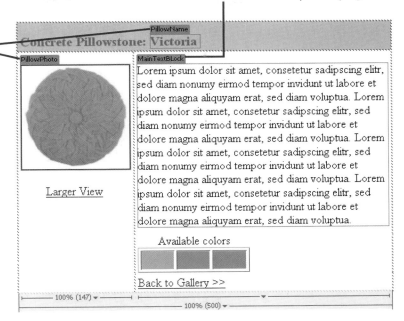

11 Save the template page and its content will appear in the upper half of the Assets tab. You can now start generating pages based on the template.

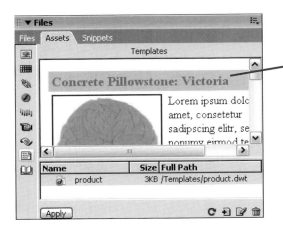

use your template

Once you create a template, you can generate as many individual pages as you need based on its design.

Choose File > New and when the New from Template dialog box appears, select the Templates tab.

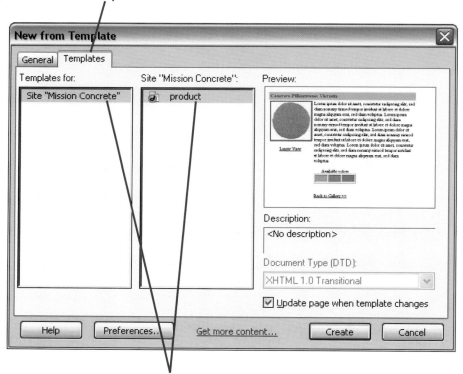

Choose your site in the first column, select the template you just created in the second column, and click Create.

reuse items to save time

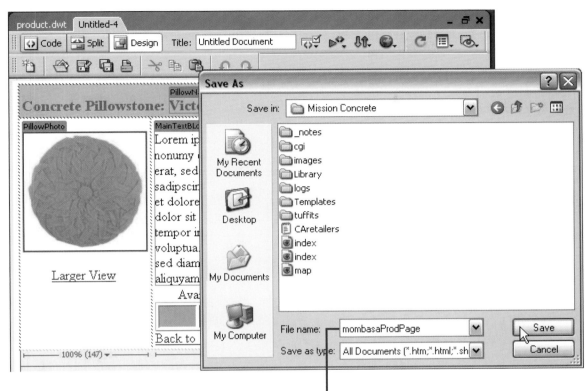

When a new untitled page based on the template appears, save it and give it a new name. (In our example, we've named the page mombasaProdpage to reflect its eventual content.) Be sure to also give the new page a title, which will be blank initially since it's a template-based page.

use your template (cont.)

You now can begin to replace the
page's editable regions, marked with
teal-colored names, with content
tailored to the individual page.

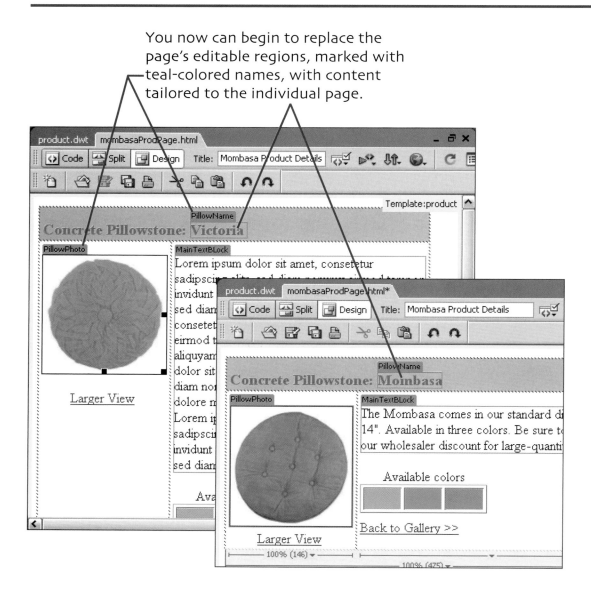

reuse items to save time

edit template

Here's the real payoff for building individual pages based on a template: You can change the template and all the pages will be updated automatically.

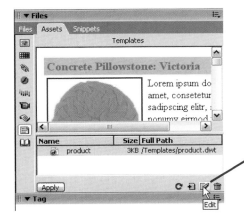

Open the template that you need to change by selecting it in the Assets tab and clicking the Edit button.

Once the template opens, make the needed changes. (In our example, we've changed the header to a color more in keeping with the Tuffits pillow palette, using the Property inspector.)

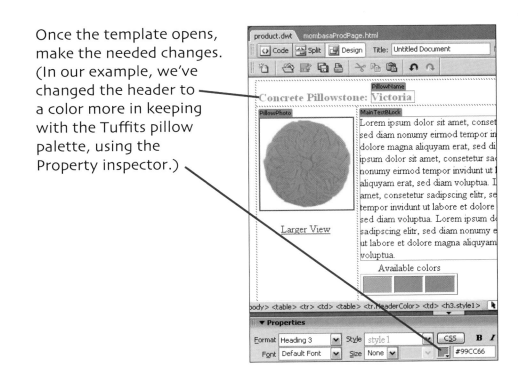

reuse items to save time

edit template (cont.)

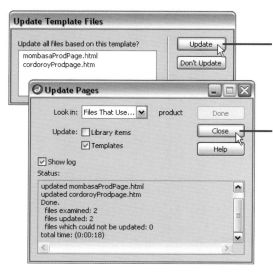

Save your changes to the template. Click Update when Dreamweaver asks if you want to change pages based on the template.

A status dialog box lists the pages updated. Click Close to apply the changes.

If you open any of the pages based on that template, you'll see that they've been updated to reflect the changes.

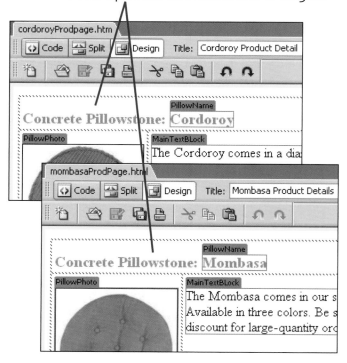

reuse items to save time

extra bits

create a library item p. 91

- The horizontal rule and copyright notice can be a single library item because they sit next to each other. If they were in two different spots on the page, they'd have to be made into two separate library items.

- While library items contain no styling themselves, they can contain references to style sheets. Use external style sheets to keep library items consistently styled, as explained on page 61.

- Dreamweaver automatically adds the .lbi suffix to a library item file name, designating the file as a library item.

create a template p. 96

- By default, every item on a template is initially locked, that is, not editable. Only the items you specifically mark as editable will be available for changes.

- When you save the template, Dreamweaver automatically adds a .dwt suffix. Dreamweaver sometimes asks if you want to update any pages using it—even though you haven't built any such pages yet. Just click Yes to close the dialog box.

reuse items to save time

8. add navigation

As your Web site grows in size, visitors need an easy way to move from page to page, or even section to section. By including a navigation bar, often called a Nav-bar, on all your pages, visitors can move around your site without getting lost.

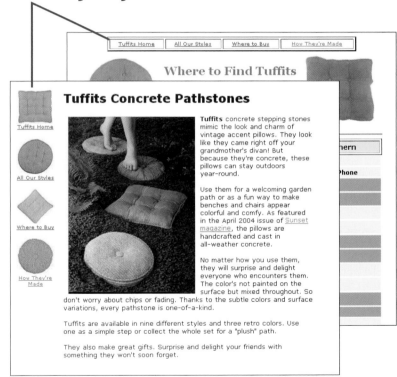

We will start by adding a Nav-bar to your site's home page. (In our example, we're adding it to the Tuffits page.) Before we add the Nav-bar, however, we're going to create two layers—one to hold the Nav-bar and one for the main area of the Web page.

add layers

Originally, Web designers were forced to use cumbersome tables or framesets to lay out magazine-style Web pages. But now that most Web browsers support style sheet positioning tags, you can use layers. In Dreamweaver, using layers is a click-and-drag affair.

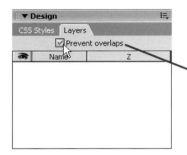

1 Switch the Insert toolbar to Layout using the drop-down menu. Press F2 to open the Layers tab of the Design panel and check Prevent overlaps.

2 Open your site's home page (in our example, the top-level tuffits page). Select the entire page (Ctrl A in Windows, ⌘ A on the Mac) and, from the Menu bar, choose Edit > Cut (Ctrl X in Windows, ⌘ X on the Mac).

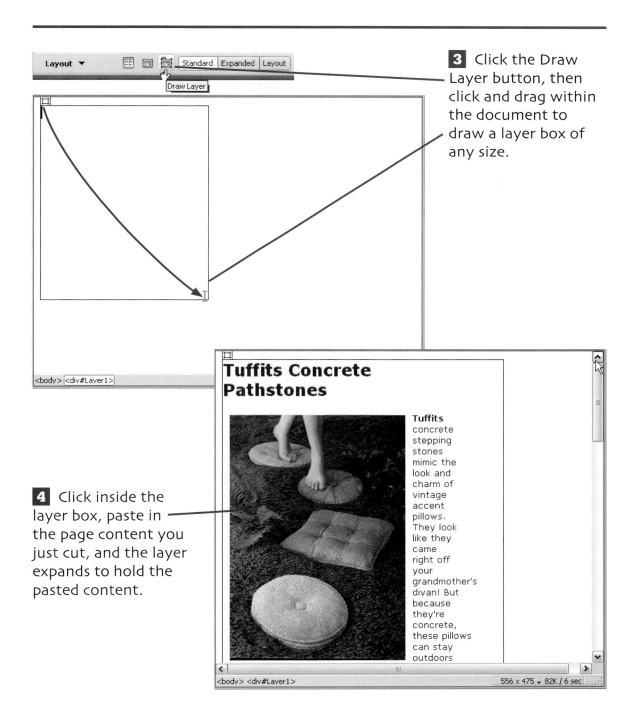

3 Click the Draw Layer button, then click and drag within the document to draw a layer box of any size.

4 Click inside the layer box, paste in the page content you just cut, and the layer expands to hold the pasted content.

add navigation

add layers (cont.)

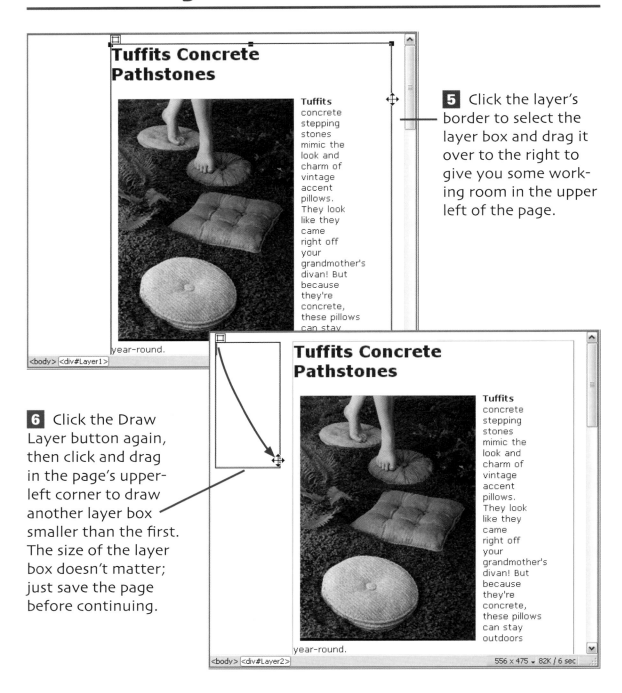

5 Click the layer's border to select the layer box and drag it over to the right to give you some working room in the upper left of the page.

6 Click the Draw Layer button again, then click and drag in the page's upper-left corner to draw another layer box smaller than the first. The size of the layer box doesn't matter; just save the page before continuing.

name layers

We're going to give these layers more meaningful names to better distinguish them from one another. (See extra bits on page 123.)

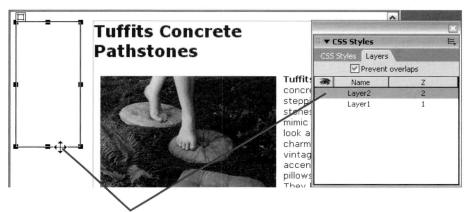

Click the left layer's border to select it and it will be highlighted in the Layers tab.

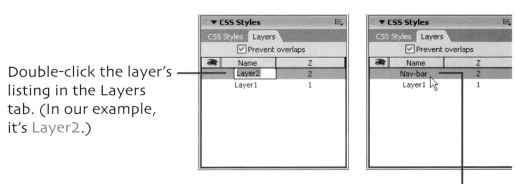

Double-click the layer's listing in the Layers tab. (In our example, it's Layer2.)

Type in a more descriptive name and press [Tab] to apply it. (In our example, we've named it Nav-bar since that's what this will become.) Select the other layer and give it a more descriptive name as well. (We'll use MainBlock.)

position layers

Now we're ready to put the layers exactly where we need them for what will become the Nav-bar. (See extra bits on page 123.)

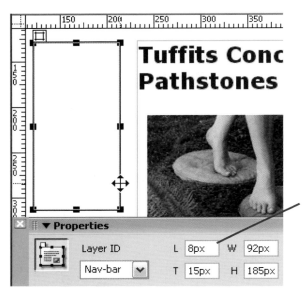

1 Make sure the Properties inspector and rulers are visible. Click to select the Nav-bar layer and take a look at two of the Properties inspector's text windows: L and T, which denote how far in px (pixels) the layer sits from the left-top corner of the page. (In our example, the layer is 8 pixels to the right and 15 pixels below the top-left corner.)

2 The absolute corner would be L: 0 and T: 0, which is where we want our Nav-bar layer to start. Type in those numbers and press Tab. The Nav-bar layer tucks itself into the top-left corner.

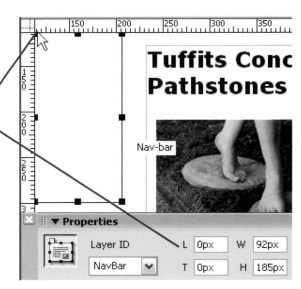

3 The W and H text windows in the Properties inspector set the layer's Width and Height. (In our example, we want the Nav-bar to be exactly 100 pixels wide, not 92 as it is on the left, and since we're not sure how high it needs to be, we'll type in 600 to be safe.)

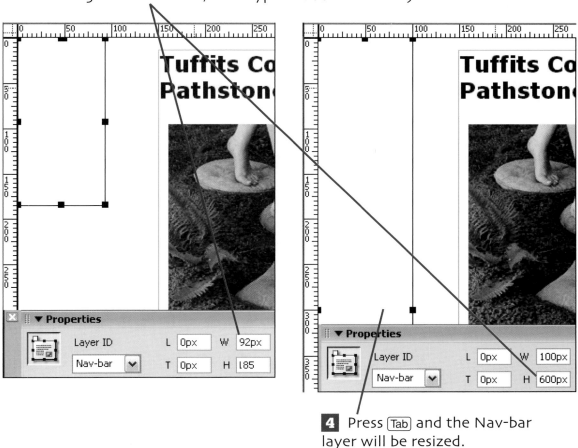

4 Press Tab and the Nav-bar layer will be resized.

position layers (cont.)

5 With the Nav-bar layer positioned, we now can put the MainBlock layer exactly where it belongs. The Nav-bar layer's L value is 0 and it's 100 pixels wide, so we'll set the MainBlock's L value at 105, which gives us a 5-pixel gutter for a bit of breathing room. Press Tab to apply the change and jump to the T text window.

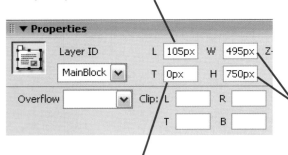

6 Like the Nav-bar layer, the MainBlock's T value should be 0 so that the layers line up across the top of the page. Press Tab to apply the change and jump to the W text window.

7 Finally, we'll set the MainBlock layer width at 495 (100 + 5 + 495 = 600, to easily fit on most monitors). Press Tab to jump to the H text window, where we'll set the height at a generous 750 pixels since Web browsers let viewers scroll down deep windows. Press Tab and you're done. Save your work before continuing.

add navigation

create main nav-bar

With the Nav-bar layer placed where we need it, adding the content is the easy part.

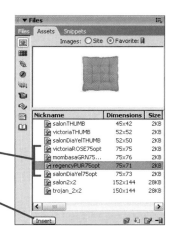

1 If you haven't already, create a series of images small enough to fit inside your new Nav-bar. (In our example, we've taken images of Tuffits pillows, reduced them to 75 pixels wide, and resampled them.)

2 Click in the Nav-bar, and click the Asset tab's Insert button. The selected image appears in the Nav-bar.

3 Right after the first Nav-bar image, add a line break, type in a short label for what will become your first text link, and then start a new paragraph. Don't bother with styling any of this just yet. Instead, repeat these steps to add the other images and link labels you need for each of your site's main areas of interest.

4 Use the Properties inspector to center the labels and images.

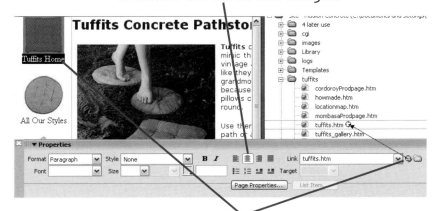

5 Since the Nav-bar's first image and text label will link to the same page, select them both and make the link using the Properties inspector.

create main nav-bar (cont.)

6 Once linked, the text immediately reflects the link colors we set in our external style sheet (mainTuffits.css) in Chapter 6. Repeat to link the rest of your Nav-bar images and text to their respective pages.

7 While the link colors look fine, the default text seems a bit big for the narrow Nav-bar. Select the first text label and use Properties inspector's drop-down menus to set the Font to Verdana, Arial, Helvetica, sans-serif and the Size to 10 pixels.

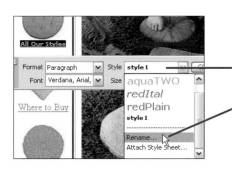

8 Dreamweaver automatically names the formatting style (in our example, it's called style1). Choose Rename from the Style drop-down menu.

add navigation

9 In the Rename Style dialog box, call the new style something that denotes its purpose (such as navbarText10) and click OK to close the dialog box.

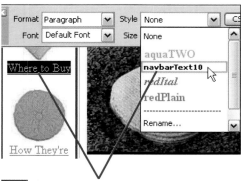

10 Apply the style to the rest of the Nav-bar text labels.

11 Now let's make the style available for other pages. In the CSS Styles tab, right-click (Windows) or Ctrl-click (Mac) the new style and choose Export from the drop-down menu. Use the dialog box that appears to save the style with the rest of your external style sheets. You can then attach that style to any page in your site, as explained on page 65.

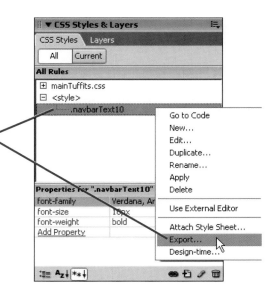

12 Before going to the next page, save your work. (From the Menu bar, choose File > Save All.)

add navigation

create small nav-bar

You could place the Nav-bar you just created on every page of the site. But in case you don't want the Nav-bar to use that much space on every page, we'll create a small, table-based Nav-bar styled much like its home-page cousin.

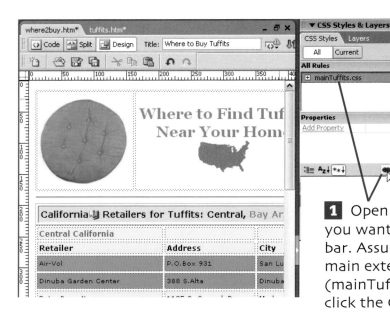

1 Open another page in which you want a compact navigation bar. Assuming it already has a main external style sheet attached (mainTuffits.css in our example), click the CSS Styles tab's Attach button.

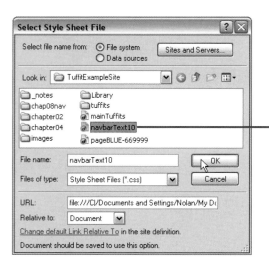

2 When the Attach External Style Sheet dialog box appears, click Browse and navigate in the Select Style Sheet File dialog box to where you saved your navbar style sheet (navbarText10 in our example). Click OK to close the Select Style Sheet File dialog box.

3 When the Attach External Style Sheet dialog box reappears, click OK to close it. The navbar style sheet (navbarText10.css) is added to the CSS Styles tab.

4 Click at the very top of the page you opened in step 1. Now click the Insert Table button in the Layout toolbar.

5 Insert a table at the very top of the page. (In our example, we inserted a 495-pixel wide table with one row and four columns, which matches the number of links in the main nav-bar.)

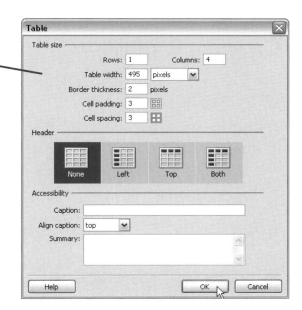

create small nav-bar (cont.)

6 Select and center the table when it appears on the page. In the table's first cell, add the text for your first link. Don't worry when the cell widths shift around as you do this.

7 Add link text to the rest of the cells, select them all, and in the Properties inspector choose NavbarText10 in the Style drop-down menu.

8 All the selected text changes to that style.

add navigation

9 Use the Properties inspector to link the text in each cell to your site's main pages.

10 As you do so, the links will be styled based on the mainTuffits style sheet already attached to the page.

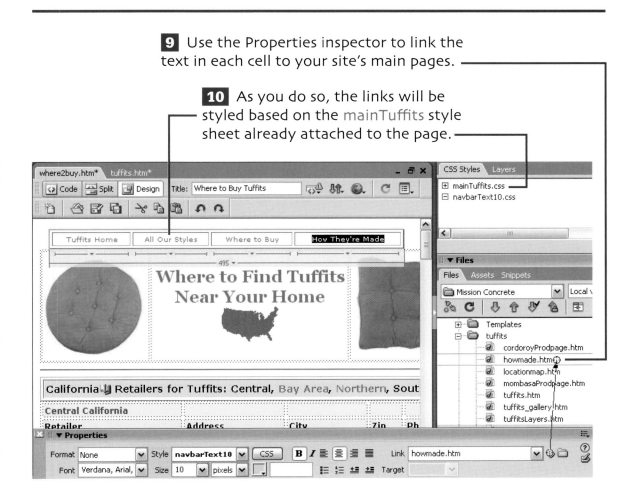

11 After you've linked all the labels in the table, save your work.

create small nav-bar (cont.)

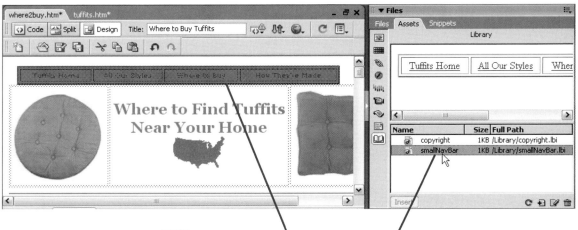

12 Select the table, turn it into a library item with a clear name (such as smallNavbar), and you'll be able to add this space-saving Nav-bar to any page.

extra bits

name layers p. 111

- You also can select a layer by clicking its name in the Layers tab.

position layers p. 112

- You also can select a layer and drag it where you want it, but for precise positioning use the Properties inspector's text windows.

9. publish site

Finally, you're ready to put your pages on the Web, a process sometimes called publishing since they'll become available for anyone to read. Dreamweaver's expanded Files panel, which displays files on the remote Web server along with those on your local machine, plays a key role in helping you keep track of which files are where and when they were last changed.

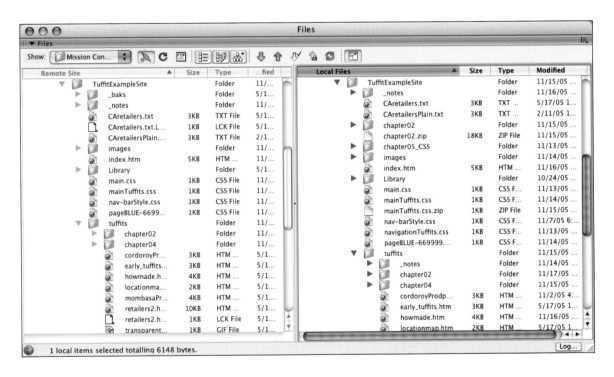

add search terms

It's easy for you to help Web search engines highlight your site if you enter a succinct description, along with multiple keywords, in the home page. Dream-weaver places this information in the page's hidden head code. (See extra bits on page 137.)

1 Open your home page and switch the Insert toolbar to HTML using the drop-down menu. Click the second button from the left and choose Keywords from its drop-down menu.

2 When the Keywords dialog box appears, type words that you think people might use to search for your site. Once you're done, click OK to close the dialog box.

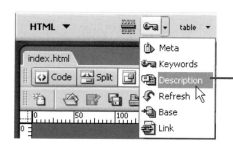

3 Click the the second button from the left again and choose Description from its drop-down menu.

4 When the Description dialog box appears, type in a short para-graph that sums up the purpose of your Web site and the products it displays. Once you're done, click OK to close the dialog box.

publish site

5 If you want to see the otherwise hidden keywords and description, click the Split button. The terms appear as part of the meta data in the page's head code.

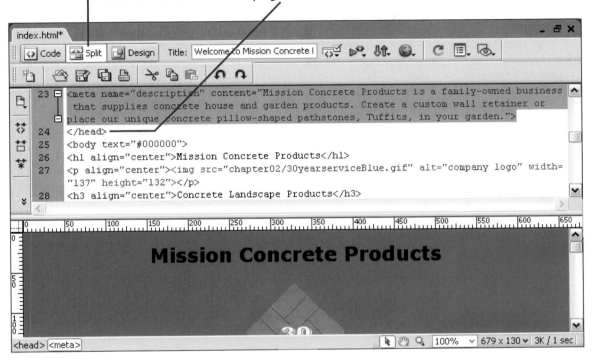

check and fix links

Few things are more frustrating for Web users than broken links. Dreamweaver can check your entire site in seconds and save everyone hours of frustration.

1 Choose Site > Check Links Sitewide. The Link Checker tab in the Results panel lists any pages with broken links. (In our example, Dreamweaver found a link we deliberately mistyped, tuffBREAK.)

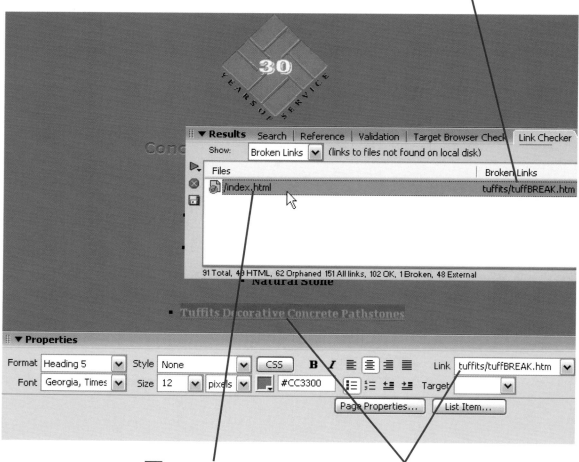

2 Double-click the file listed and Dreamweaver opens the Properties inspector, along with the page that contains the broken link.

3 Use the Properties inspector's Link text field to correct the mistake by typing in the correct link or redrawing the link with the Point to File icon.

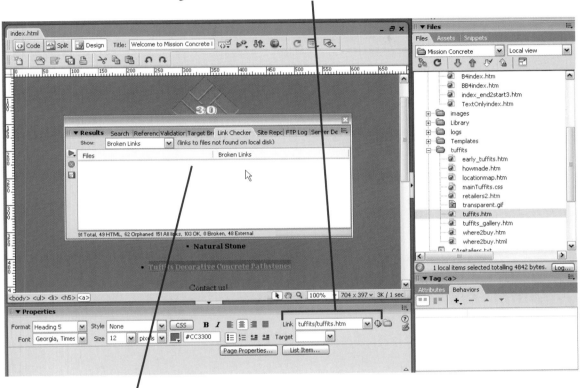

4 Once you make the fix, save the page and the Results panel automatically removes the previously broken link from its list. Repeat until you've fixed all broken links.

explore the files panel

The Files panel serves as your main tool to put files from your local site on to the remote Web site. You also use it to get any of your remote files if, for example, you've accidentally deleted their local site counterparts. (See extra bits on page 137.)

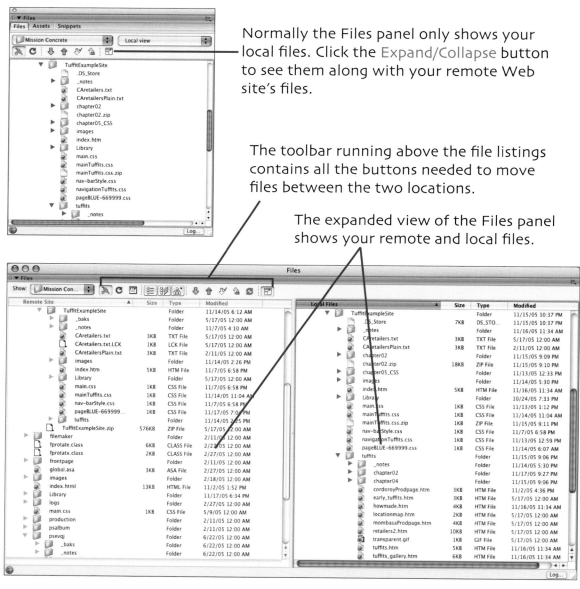

Normally the Files panel only shows your local files. Click the Expand/Collapse button to see them along with your remote Web site's files.

The toolbar running above the file listings contains all the buttons needed to move files between the two locations.

The expanded view of the Files panel shows your remote and local files.

publish site

Click the
Connect/Disconnect
button to open or close
a live connection to the
remote Web site.

Click the Get files
button to move
selected files from
the remote site to
the local site.

Click the Put files
button to move
selected files from
your local site to
the remote site.

Click the Refresh
button after moving
files in either direc-
tion to update the
file listings.

Do not use these two buttons
unless you're working with a
group of people and have
activated Dreamweaver's
check-in/check-out file system.

The Expand/Collapse button
lets you see the remote and
local files, or just the local files.

publish site

connect to remote site

After double-checking your files, you're ready to place them on your remote site. Since you already entered the remote site's address details back in Chapter 1, you're ready to connect. (See extra bits on page 137.)

1 Unless you have an always-on connection to the Internet, activate your computer's dial-up connection now.

2 Return to Dreamweaver, make sure the Files panel is visible, and click the Expand/Collapse button.

3 Once the view expands, click the Connect button.

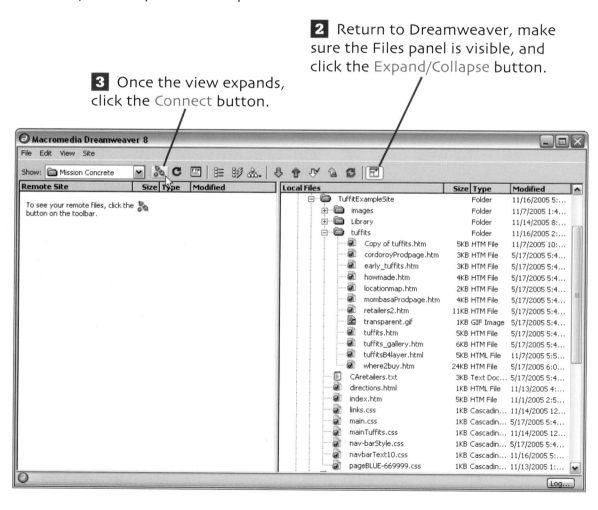

4 The Status dialog box appears briefly as Dreamweaver negotiates the connection to your Web site.

5 Once the connection is made, the remote site's files appears in the left side of the Files panel. (In our example, we haven't put any files on the site yet, so all you see is the top-level folder, webdocs, and two don't-touch subfolders, cgi and logs.)

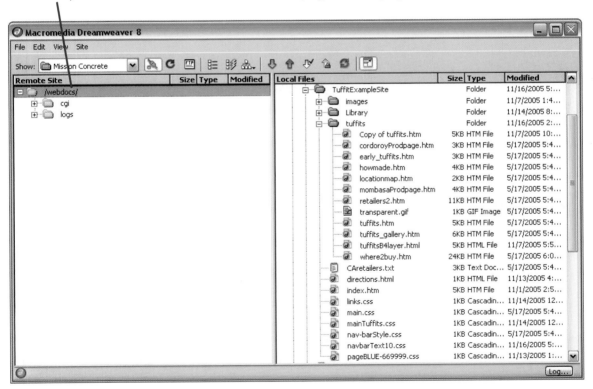

6 You're ready to upload your files.

publish site

upload multiple files

If this is the first upload to your Web site, you'll be publishing multiple files, including all the necessary images for your pages. (See extra bits on page 137.)

1 Select the home page, index, in the Local Files pane and click the Put button to begin the upload.

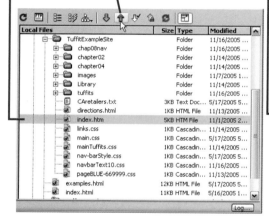

You also can select individual files or folders by Ctrl-clicking (Windows) or ⌘-clicking (Mac) them in the Local Files pane. Click the Put button to upload them.

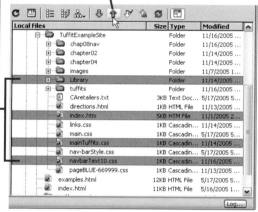

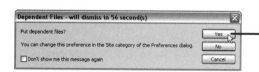

2 When Dreamweaver asks if you want to include dependent files, click Yes. Dependent files include every file and image linked, directly or indirectly, to the selected page(s). (In our example, this would include not only the index page, but also the attached main. Tuffits.css style sheet.)

3 A series of progress dialog boxes flash by as Dreamweaver uploads the home page and all its dependent files. This may take several minutes to complete, depending on how many files you're uploading and the speed of your Internet connection.

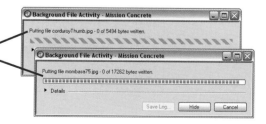

4 When the progress dialog boxes stop appearing, press the Refresh button...

5 ...and then compare names of the Remote Site files to the names of your Local Files.

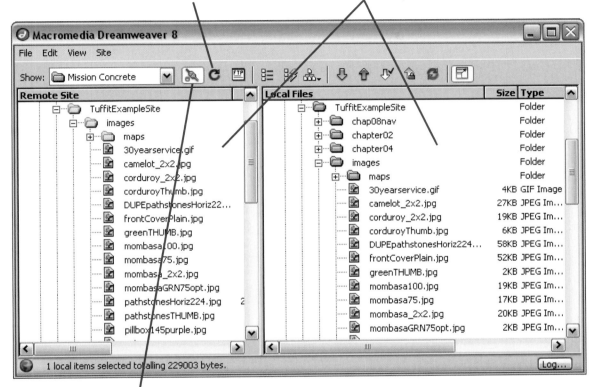

6 Check how the remote site pages look in your Web browser to make sure their appearance matches that of your local files. If you find mismatches, upload the local files again.

7 Once you're done, click the Disconnect button.

upload a single page

Sometimes you'll need to upload only a single page—for example, when you need to update information or fix a mistake. (See extra bits on page 137.)

1 Once you're connected, click the page file in the Local Files pane and drag it to the folder where the older version appears in the Remote Site pane.

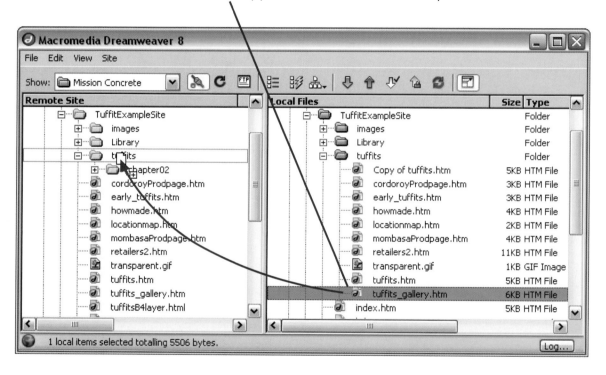

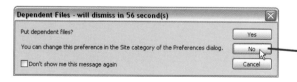

2 When Dreamweaver asks if you want to include dependent files, click No. A single progress dialog box appears as Dreamweaver uploads the selected page. Use your Web browser to check the page on the remote Web site, and when you're done, click the Disconnect button.

extra bits

add search terms p. 126

- When picking keywords and a description, especially for an uncommon product or service, think of similar products or services and use words people would most likely type in to find them.

explore the files panel p. 130

- If you are working solo, the check-in/check-out system is cumbersome since it forces you to alert yourself that you're using a file.

- Sometimes it's tough to make room on the screen for a good view of your Web pages and the full Files panel, even on a large monitor. The easiest workaround is to arrange both just as you want them and press [F8] to toggle the Files panel on or off.

connect to remote site p. 132

- The local and remote versions of the cgi and logs folders are different since they reflect the specific activities for each set of files. If you try to replace one with the other, Dreamweaver cancels the transfer.

upload multiple files p. 134

- While you could select your local site's top-level folder (in this case, TuffitExampleSite) and upload the whole thing, it's not recommended. You run the risk of publishing files you're still working on, not to mention wiping out remote files not found on your local site. Instead, it's best to upload only the local files and folders you specifically select.

upload a single page p. 136

- Since you've only changed the HTML file, there's no need to upload the dependent files that are already on the remote site.

index

index

index

index

index

Sharpen button, 34, 41
sharpen slider, 41
shortcuts, keyboard, 8
shortcuts bar, 31
Show Grid command, 48
showing/hiding
  Insert toolbar, 2
  panels, 8
  Properties inspector, 3
Site Definition windows, 5–7, 8
Site radio button, 90
Size menu, 24, 28
Smith, Dori, xiv
Snap To Grid command, 48
Snippets tab, 8
Sort Table dialog box, 58, 60
sorting data, ix, 58–59, 60
special characters, 12, 13, 31
Split button, 127
Split view, 2
spreadsheet data, 54
Standard button, 48
Standard toolbar, 2
Start Page, 4, 10
Status dialog box, 133
Studio, Macromedia, xiii
Style menu, 24
style sheets, 61–74
  adding CSS rules to, 69–71
  applying to single page, 74
  attaching to Web page, 65–68, 74
  creating, 62–64, 74
  creating custom rules for, 72–73
  editing, 74
  naming, 74
  purpose of, 61
subfolders, 45

T

tab-separated text, 54
table-based Nav-bars, 118–22
Table dialog box, 49, 52, 60
table headers, 49, 52–53, 60
<table> tag, 60
Table Widths option, 48

tables, 47–60
  adding images to, 50–51
  adding to Web page, 48–49
  aligning, 48
  aligning text in, 71
  displaying width of, 48
  editing, 56
  importing data into, 54–55, 60
  inserting horizontal rule in, 51
  labeling rows/columns in, 49, 52–53, 60
  merging cells in, 53
  as page-layout tool, 47, 48
  resizing, 60
  selecting, 60
  setting options for, 48
  sorting data in, ix, 58–59, 60
  using color in, ix, 57, 60
Tabular Data icon, 54
tag selector, 15, 16, 17
Target menu, 78, 88
Target text box, Properties inspector, 34
<td> tag, 69
templates, 96–104
  creating, 96–99
  editing, 103–4
  file suffix for, 105
  generating Web pages based on, 100–102
  marking editable regions in, 98, 105
  naming, 96
  purpose of, 96
  saving, 99, 105
Test Connection button, 7
testing
  links, 77, 87
  online connection, 7, 8
text
  adding to home page, 12–13
  aligning images with, 44
  formatting, 22
  size considerations, 31
  wrapping around images, 34, 42–43, 45
text labels, 44
text links, 76–78, 88
Text setting, shortcuts bar, 31
text size, 31
thumbnail images, 40

tiled images, 21
Times font, 28
Times New Roman font, 28
timesavers, 89
titles, page, 10, 11, 31, 48, 101
toolbars, 2, 8
triangle-shaped arrow, 8

U

< ul > tag, 29
Undo Crop command, 37
Unordered List icon, 20
unordered lists, 20, 29–30
uploading files, 134–36, 137
URL, 5

V

V Space text box, 43, 45
Verdana font, 24, 26
views, 2, 8
Visual QuickProject Guides, vii
Visual QuickStart Guides, xiv
visually impaired visitors, 34, 45, 60

W

Web browsers
    checking remote site pages in, 135, 136
    and layers, 108, 114
    and library items, 95
    and page titles, 31
    and style sheet positioning tags, 108
    testing links in, 77, 82, 87
    for visually impaired visitors, 45, 60
Web-hosting firms, 7, 8
Web page. See also home page; Web site
    adding images to, 35–36
    adding layers to, 108–10
    adding tables to, 48–49

Web page (continued)
    adding text to, 12–13, 31
    adding title to, 10, 11, 48
    attaching style sheet to, 65–68, 74
    building from template, 96–102
    creating, 10–11
    creating CSS rules for, 22–30, 32
    creating headings for, 16–18, 24–28, 32
    creating lists for, 19–20
    displaying as tab, 31
    inserting image placeholders in, 14–15
    linking to. See links
    linking to specific spot in, 83–84
    naming, 11, 31
    reusing items on, 89
    saving, 11, 13
    setting page background for, 21
    updating based on template, 103–4
    uploading, 136
Web site. See also Web page
    adding Nav-bar to, 107, 115–22
    checking for broken links, 128–29
    collaborating on, 8
    connecting to, 132–33
    creating home page for. See home page
    creating links between pages in, 76–77
    helping search engines find, 126–27
    keeping track of files for, 125
    publishing, 125–37
    reusing items on, 89
    setting up local version of, 4–8
    this book's companion, xii
    viewing files for, 3
Windows system
    keyboard shortcuts, 8
    text size on, 31
wrapping text, 34, 42–43, 45

XML, 31